Common Goldfish

Other titles in this series

The Tropical Aquarium
Community Fishes
Marine Fishes
The Healthy Aquarium
Garden Ponds
Koi
Fancy Goldfishes
Livebearing Fishes
African Cichlids
Fish Breeding
Aquarium Plants

An INTERPET Guide to

Coldwater Fishes

Shubunkins

Red Fantails

An INTERPET Guide to

Coldwater Fishes

A comprehensive survey of coldwater fishes suitable for keeping in aquariums and ponds, including Koi Carp

Dick Mills

INTERPET

An **INTERPET** Book

Vincent Lane, Dorking,
Surrey RH4 3YX,
United Kingdom.

ISBN 1-902389-53-0

This reprint 2005

Red Oranda

Credits

Editor: Geoff Rogers
Designer: Tony Dominy
Colour reproductions:
Tempus Litho and Pixel Tech Ltd.
Filmset: SX Composing DTP
Printed in China by Leefung Asco Printers Ltd.

Author

The author, Dick Mills, has been keeping fishes for over 30 years, during which time he has written many articles for aquatic hobby magazines as well as over a dozen books. A member of his local aquarist society, for the past 25 years he has also been a council member of the Federation of British Aquatic Societies, for which he regularly lectures and produces a quarterly news magazine.

Consultant

Fascinated by fishkeeping from early childhood, Dr. Neville Carrington devised an internationally known liquid food for young fishes while studying for a pharmacy degree. After obtaining his Doctorate in Pharmaceutical Engineering Science and a period in industry, Dr. Carrington has pursued a life-long interest in developing equipment and chemical products for the aquarium world.

Contents

Coldwater fishkeeping is the oldest by far of the three main areas of the aquarium hobby. This should not be a surprising fact, for Man became interested in fish (for food) and fishkeeping (for pleasure) long before the discovery of electricity led to the now taken-for-granted ease of tropical fishkeeping.

Despite its apparent narrowness of appeal, the coldwater aquarium has much to offer: the fishes can cover a wide range of sizes and colours often exceeding those in the tropical field; and there is a very great opportunity for line-breeding, and the search for the 'perfect' specimen is always being under taken by a coldwater fishkeeper somewhere.

A few years ago, the term 'coldwater fishes' was usually understood to mean Goldfishes, but nowadays there is a greater awareness of the many other species that can be kept in unheated

aquariums, thus widening the scope of coldwater fishkeeping.

Fishes from all temperate zones of the world can be kept successfully in captivity without expensive thermostatically controlled heating equipment. They are usually more hardy and offer just as much interest in their breeding methods – and present just as many challenges as tropical fishes!

The interest is not confined to indoors: coldwater fishkeeping can be undertaken outside, possibly coupled with that other great interest, gardening; and the combination of the two can result in an end product of truly breathtaking beauty.

Specialist societies now cater for serious Goldfish, Koi and North American Native fishkeepers, a sure pointer to the continuing popularity of this side of the hobby, which regrettably most people only associate with the Goldfish in its humble, unsuitable bowl.

Aquarium or pond?

The potential is so great when considering taking up coldwater fishkeeping, that you should first ask yourself where your interests lie – not only at the present, but where they might expand to in the future. Much depends on what stage in life you are at, as finances and property ownership also have a certain bearing on what decision you eventually take. You might even be thinking of coldwater fishkeeping because you are not confident in your skills in coping with the technicalities of tropical fishes.

To take a well-known set of events first: you happen to obtain a Goldfish through the usual channels – either at a pet shop or at a fair (always assuming you can get the hoop-la ring over the bowl!). It is unlikely that you will have immediate plans to re-landscape the garden to accommodate a large pond, and so the fish becomes destined for an aquarium in the house somewhere. It is true that the coldwater aquarium is generally bigger than its tropical counterpart and, strangely, that it usually contains less fishes, but an aquarium of up to 1.5m (5ft) in length is not beyond the space available in most homes.

Another example: you have bought your own house and want to add some movement and water to the garden. Now is the time to consider a pool seriously, but what type of pool? Is your garden large enough for a formal pool, or will it be a small prefabricated affair alongside a rockery in that corner that you've always wanted to brighten up? Installing a pool of any size involves hard manual work, particularly in clearing the site, and digging the hole or constructing a brick-built free-standing pool.

Indoor and outdoor aquariums both have their advantages and disadvantages. The garden pool is not at its best all the year round, and even in summer there may be days when the weather is hardly suitable for fish-watching. The indoor aquarium is watchable in all weathers, and may be quite satisfactory at first, but when the hobby begins to take over and more tanks are needed, the rest of the family might not share your enthusiasm quite so much!

Indoor and outdoor fishes

What types of fishes can you keep indoors? The answer is almost any, providing you can find room for their aquarium, but generally the fishes do not exceed 20cm (8in) in size. Within this limitation are practically all the Goldfishes including the very many fancy varieties, the smaller wild fishes and juvenile forms of those larger species that are normally regarded as pool fish.

Fishes for outdoors include some of those normally kept in aquariums, but they will grow bigger in the larger environment of a pool. Large fishes such as Koi and Golden Orfe are easily seen from the poolside, as are the bigger Goldfishes, but some of the native species may be too small or will dwell on the bottom of the pool far from the gaze of their keeper. In any case, the more delicate varieties of Goldfishes must be brought back indoors during the winter months as they cannot survive the cold.

First decisions

Thinking in terms of sheer practicabilities, most people begin with the indoor aquarium before extending their aquatic interest out into the garden, or even into a fishhouse where extra breeding tanks can be accommodated without taking up valuable living space in the house. On the other hand, you may find yourself inheriting a garden pool on moving house; this book is designed to give you a detailed look at the many fishes that can be successfully kept in either pool or aquarium, whether for purely decorative pleasure or as a serious hobby.

Before plunging into any actual fishkeeping, remember that both indoor and outdoor fishkeeping have advantages and disadvantages; it is well worth studying both systems before committing yourself.

Right: *Indoor or outdoor? Study the accompanying table to see which system – pond or aquarium – suits your requirements the best.*

AQUARIUM	POND
Convenient and self-contained.	Away from house, needs electricity supply and drainage system.
Can be installed very quickly.	Planning and installation often very protracted if started at wrong time of year; also dependent on weather conditions.
Size of fishes limited.	Large fishes may be kept.
All fishes easy to see.	Some species not seen at all.
Requires certain amount of artificial aids – filtration, aeration, etc. Live foods must be supplied by aquarist.	Benefits by natural action of climate, and supply of live foods (insects).
Can be messy when water changes due.	Pool maintenance causes less upheaval to household.
Fishes safe from predators.	Fishes must be guarded from cats and herons.
Fishes easy to catch.	Fishes more difficult to catch.
Installation must allow for easy maintenance but also compatibility with interior furnishing.	Blends in quite naturally with garden surroundings. Marginal plants can help assimilation into garden features.
Special arrangements need to be made if breeding is intended.	Fishes breed naturally, although provision must be made to collect eggs or fry.
Water conditions can be easily controlled and monitored.	Water conditions affected by contaminated rain, garden sprays, etc.
Diseases easily seen, diagnosed and treated.	If disease is suspected, fish must be removed at best, or whole pool treated or drained at worst.
Lighting and plant growth can be controlled.	Position of pool critical to avoid excessive sunshine or leaves from trees.
Aquatic plants limited to a few species.	More plants suitable for pools.

Selecting a tank

The qualities of an aquarium are different to the fishkeeper than to the fishes that live within it.

All the fishkeeper requires of a tank is that it holds water, looks smart and doesn't cost too much! The fishes require living space, it is true, but the design of the tank is critical for a far more important reason, as we shall see in this section of the book.

The correct design of tank

It must be stated at the outset that the goldfish bowl is entirely unsuitable for keeping fishes, so our attention has to turn to rectangular tanks. These used to be made of angle-iron frames with glass panels set in putty. Despite the best of attentions to prevent rusting, either by galvanizing the frames or by coating them with nylon or plastic, time eventually brought their downfall with the inevitable rust, and the puttied glass panels were liable to leak (particularly after the tank had been emptied and moved).

The modern aquarium is an all-glass construction, with glass panels bonded together with silicone rubber adhesive. (One-piece tanks, made from moulded clear plastic or similar materials, are also available but not readily obtainable in the sizes required for coldwater fishes.) Because we can now bond sheets of glass directly to each other, it is possible to make a fish tank of almost any conceivable shape or size; but although that empty corner of the room could well be filled by a triangular tank, we shall concentrate here on rectangular shapes – for one thing, some necessary arithmetical calculations (which we shall have to use shortly) will be so much easier!

Tanks are commercially available in 'standard' sizes; both lengths and breadths are usually in multiples of 30cm (12in). The depth ranges from 30cm (12in) to 60cm (24in); 38cm (15in) is favoured as the average depth for aquariums 60cm (24in) to 90cm (36in) long because it gives a better-proportioned underwater 'picture'. For a coldwater aquarium, a tank 60cm (24in) long should be regarded as the *minimum* size, with 90cm (36in) or 1m (39in) as the preferred length where possible.

The problem of leaking tanks has practically been overcome with the use of silicone rubber sealant, but all tanks should be checked for leaks before use. This should be done out of doors for two reasons. The first is obvious – who wants a mess indoors? The second reason is that if the leak is to be repaired, it is best done in well-ventilated conditions, as the sealant gives off a heavy vapour. Although many of the sealants on the market will actually do the job, it is advisable that only aquarium-suitable sealants are used; many of the others contain a mildew retardant that could prove fatal to the fishes.

All-glass tanks of 1m (39in) length and over tend to bow outwards under the pressure of water, and such tanks usually have a bracing bar across the top to reduce this tendency. Decorative 'angled edging' of anodized metal may enhance the appearance but this is simply stuck to the outside of the glass and hardly contributes to the tank's strength, although it does add protection to (and from) the otherwise vulnerable bare glass edges. More decorative trim is added to the cover or reflector hood, and the whole aquarium can harmonize artistically with even the most ultra-modern home furnishings. So much for the fishkeeper's needs of a tank; how about those of the fish?

How many fishes?

Through their gills fishes absorb oxygen dissolved in the aquarium water and convert it to carbon dioxide. A good supply of oxygen is therefore most important. Although cool water can hold more oxygen than warm water, coldwater fishes do require more than tropical fishes and generally grow larger; this means that conditions governing the supply of oxygen to the water are vital.

The oxygen in the water converted by fishes can be replaced in any considerable amounts only by atmospheric oxygen entering the water at the surface; hence the aquarium should have a large surface area. Looking at it another way, each 2.5cm (1in) of fish body length should have approximately 150cm^2 (24in^2) of water surface allocated to it.

If our tank has a length of 1m (39in) and a width (front to back) of 30cm (12in) it has a surface area of 3,000cm^2 (468in^2), so it can comfortably hold around 50cm (20in) of fish. The depth of water is not taken into consideration during these calculations; it just means that in deeper tanks the fishes have more swimming room.

This is now the accepted method of 'sizing' a fish tank for its inhabitants, and is more accurate then the out-moded 'X litres (gallons) for each Y centimetres (inches) of fish' method, which disregards the crucial factor of the water surface area.

Just as important as renewing the oxygen supply through the water surface is the expulsion of carbon dioxide (exhaled by the fishes), which again can occur only at the water surface.

During the hours of darkness, carbon dioxide is produced as part of both fish and plant respiratory cycles, although during the daytime (or 'tanklight') plants actually consume carbon dioxide. A large water surface area will help to dissipate this unwanted gas from the aquarium, and we shall see in following sections how gaseous exchange can be increased in other ways.

Tank location

The location of the tank is important for several reasons. The site should be strong enough to support the weight of the full and furnished tank, and a very firm, level foundation is required. Any unevenness in the surface on which the tank stands can be covered by a thick piece of expanded polystyrene sheeting: this will prevent stresses being set up which otherwise might result in a cracked glass panel, with disastrous results. The aquarium should not be located near a window facing the sun: not only is there a risk of the water overheating, but also this situation, with its uncontrolled amount of light, will encourage the growth of algae.

The coldwater aquarium wlll, paradoxically, require access to a power outlet; unlike its tropical counterpart the aquarium does not need heating, but it will require power for the lighting, aeration and filtration equipment. This is another factor to consider when locating the tank.

Below: *Fish-holding capacities of a goldfish bowl (keep the water level to the widest part) and two tanks of similar volume. The largest surface area supports the highest number of fishes, irrespective of water depth.*

Tank furnishings

The furnishing of an aquarium is a very subjective affair, with no two fishkeepers likely to produce the same end result for similar fishes. Again, there has to be a balance between what the fishkeeper wants and what the fishes require.

Tank furnishings include the gravel bed, rocks, logs, bark, twisted roots and other tank decorations of inert or artificial materials.

Aquarium gravel

Although a bed of gravel is not altogether necessary for the plants (which could be grown just as well in pots), the indoor aquarium takes on a more pleasing appearance if the tank floor is covered with a landscaped gravel bed. The size and constitution of the gravel are also important.

If the particle size is too small, plants will have difficulty rooting and biological filtration systems may be disrupted: but if the particle size is too large, then uneaten food many fall between them and rot away, causing pollution of the aquarium. A particle size of approximately 3mm (0.1in) is about right.

The composition of the gravel could alter the water chemistry if it contains excessive amounts of calcium. There are coloured gravels available for aquarium use, but these are slightly risky because the colour may leak out into the water; it is probably safer to stick to the normal mid-brown/yellow colour of the standard aquarium gravel sold by your local dealer.

The use of rocks

Rocks in the coldwater aquarium are primarily used for dramatic effect, unlike the tropical aquarium, where many of the species may be rock-dwellers by nature. Inert, non-soluble rocks should be used – slate, granite, basalt or quartz – and care should be taken to select only well-worn pieces, so that the fishes do not injure themselves on any sharp edges. Small round pebbles can be advantageously used around the

Below: *Gravel particles of around 3mm (0.1in) are best for the aquarium; use this natural colour.*

Above left: *In this fully furnished aquarium the rockwork adds a welcome dimension and also serves to protect the plant roots from the foraging activities of the fishes.*

Above: *The logs and stones in the foreground maintain the slope of the gravel and hold the cork bark down. Aquarium plants can be arranged in terraces for a stunning effect.*

roots of aquarium plants: Goldfishes are great scavengers and the pebbles will prevent the plants being constantly uprooted by the fishes' foraging actions.

A method of using rock without taking up too much tank space is to glue pieces of rock directly on to the sides and rear wall of the tank with sealant; similarly, small outcrops of rocks can be fashioned and stuck together as a unit before placing in the aquarium.

Wood and cork bark

A very natural tank decoration is wood, and a suitable root or log will enhance the aquarium's appearance greatly. Bogwood, petrified wood and driftwood are all suitable for use, if certain precautions are taken. The wood used should be long dead, with no sign of rotting away. Boil it in successive changes of water and then keep it submerged, again in changes of water, until all tendency to float, or to release colour into the water, ceases. Alternatively, wood can be given several sealing coats of polyurethane varnish, which will render it safe for aquarium use.

Another natural substance used by many fishkeepers as tank decoration is cork bark. It is quite workable and forms a very beautiful backdrop to the aquarium; but make sure that no fishes can get behind it and become trapped.

Both wood and cork have a natural tendency to float but they can be persuaded to retain the position chosen for them by tying them down to a gravel-filled bottle or pipe, or by fixing them to a plate buried beneath the aquarium gravel.

Artificial decorations

Mention must be made of artificial aquarium decorations. These range from unrealistic sunken galleons (complete with mermaids and divers) and terraced walls to completely realistic logs, roots and plants. The only facility that the artificial plants lack is their absorption of carbon dioxide; apart from this, they soon become covered with a light layer of algae and are hard to distinguish from the real thing. They also have one real advantage – fishes cannot eat them!

Aeration and air pumps

Closely allied to the fishes' need for an adequate supply of oxygen, is the problem of keeping conditions clean in a closed system such as the aquarium; is the aquarist's duty to prevent it becoming a stagnant body of water, with all the horrors that such a description conjures up.

The value of aeration

Despite what newcomers to fishkeeping may think, aeration does not aid the absorption of oxygen into the water by the physical force of the bubbles, nor is much oxygen absorbed from the bubbles as they rise through the water.

The value of aeration lies in the turbulence and water movement that it causes. By constantly moving the water, usually in a turning over action, aeration brings the lower water levels to the top, where absorption of oxygen and the expellation of carbon dioxide is encouraged at the water surface. It has to be acknowledged that aeration effectively increases the apparent surface area of the tank, and to many fishkeepers this means only one thing – the ability of the tank to hold more fishes. This state of affairs holds good only as long as the aeration system remains in perfect working order; should it fail, then the tank's fish-holding capacity reverts to that governed by the dimensions of the tank and the fishes will soon find themselves gasping for breath.

Aeration is an excellent aid to help things along even better, particularly in the coldwater aquarium during the warm summer months, when the water's oxygen-carrying capacity falls. Should you now have become disillusioned about aeration, don't be too downhearted; the air pump probably produces air over and above what is necessary for straightforward aeration, which can be put to other uses.

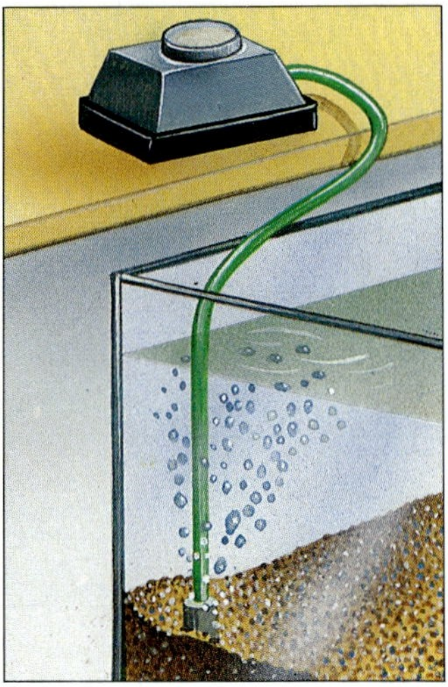

Above: *Site the air pump above the water level if possible to prevent water siphoning back into the pump should it or the electricity supply fail.*

Air pumps

The modern air pump is reliable and even the most modest model will provide enough air for the requirements of a single aquarium. The more expensive pumps may be more powerful and quieter, but there is little point in spending unnecessarily large sums of money at the outset, until you know whether you are going to need a large amount of air or not.

The air pump should be situated above the water level if possible, to avoid water siphoning back into the

Left: *The movement of air bubbles from the airstone (diffuser) continuously brings water from the bottom to the top of the aquarium, where oxygen can be replenished and carbon dioxide expelled.*

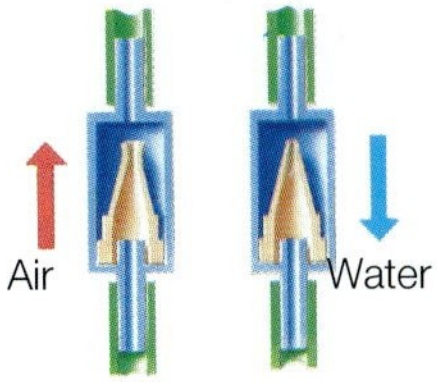

Above: *The tip of the one-way check valve opens to allow air through, but closes to prevent water reaching the pump should it stop.*

Left: *Where the pump is sited below the water level use a one-way check valve in the airline to prevent back-siphoning. An 'anti-siphon' loop in the airline above the tank also performs the same function.*

pump if the electricity supply to the pump fails; but in practice, most fishkeepers site the air pump on a convenient shelf alongside or below the aquarium and in these circumstances precautions should be taken to safeguard the pump against water damage. Either the airline to the aquarium should be looped a few centimetres above the waterline, or alternatively a check valve (which allows air to pass only one way) should be fitted into the air supply line between the pump and the control valves, fairly close to the pump connection.

A convenient method of regulating the air supply to the various pieces of aquarium equipment is by means of a group of valves. These are ganged together and fixed to the outside of the aquarium by a sticky pad; each appliance can then be independently controlled.

Maintenance of air pumps is not overdemanding, and involves only periodic cleaning of the air filter (situated beneath the body of the pump) and of the air valves in the pump mechanism. After long periods of use the diaphragm in vibrator-type pumps may split, but replacements are easy to obtain and to fix. Piston-type pumps require regular lubrication, and in addition to the check valve, an oil filter should be incorporated into the air supply line to prevent oil from entering the tank.

Below: *A cutaway of a modern air pump showing the electromagnetic coil which causes the diaphragm to pulse 50 times per second and thus pump air.*

Filtration

Filtration systems are especially necessary in the coldwater aquarium, where the constant foraging habits of species such as the Goldfish produce a permanent mistiness of suspended material in the water. The long-finned varieties of Fancy Goldfish require very clean water conditions if their fins are not to be attacked by bacteria, which are encouraged by poor water conditions.

It is apparent that the water will soon lose some of its original clarity as the fishes move around stirring things up, but other factors are involved too. As well as the fishes' obvious waste products, there are some invisible waste products too, which must be removed from the aquarium or their effects kept to a minimum.

Ammonia-based substances (excreted by the fishes during respiration) will build up to toxic levels if not controlled, and a layer of rotting detritus on the aquarium floor is neither pleasant to look at nor particularly conducive to healthy fishes. Efficient filtration of the water (coupled with conscientious tank management by the fishkeeper) will do much to keep the aquarium and its inhabitants healthy.

Aquarium filter designs

Filters are of three kinds: mechanical, chemical and biological. Mechanical filters simply remove suspended material by trapping it in fairly dense material contained in a box through which the aquarium waste is passed. Within the box, other materials (such as activated carbon) will remove dissolved materials from the water. Thus most mechanical filters are also chemical filters.

The ammonia-based compounds are removed by a biological filter, which is a device for encouraging a colony of bacteria in a gravel bed through which the water is drawn. The process of rendering the toxic compounds safe is in two stages: *Nitrosomonas* bacteria convert the ammonia to a substance known as nitrite, and this in turn is converted into nitrate by *Nitrobacter* bacteria. By using the natural method of denitrifying bacteria, both ammonia and nitrite (each toxic to fishes) have been changed to a less harmful compound, nitrate, which can be used by plants as a food source. The bacteria colony is encouraged to develop in the gravel bed in the aquarium by causing oxygenated water to flow through it. Undergravel filter systems differ in design, but the basic principle remains the same.

What type of filter to use?

Mechanical filters are probably the most widely used, although biological filters are gaining in popularity as the resistance to their use (by fishkeepers who do not fully understand their

Right: *Undergravel filters may be operated by choosing either an air pump or a powerhead. The powerhead arrangement is illustrated here. A powerhead provides an additional benefit for the aquarium in that it has a higher flow rate.*

Below and below right: *Position the undergravel filter plates so that they cover the entire base of the tank. Put them in place before you add the gravel. Then assemble the uplift tubes and slot them into position in one or both rear corners. To power them, attach airlines and airstones as directed by the manufacturer. Finally, add an even layer of well-washed aquarium gravel over the surface of the whole filter plate.*

workings in theory or in practice) is overcome. Mechanical filters should be large enough to process the relatively large volume of water in the selected aquarium size (1m/39in long). Whether to use an inside or an outside model depends on how you utilize the aquarium.

A purely decorative aquarium should be serviced by an outside filter so that the regular necessary maintenance does not upset the furnishings and plants in the tank. An aquarium used for the raising of young fishes, however, where growth is the all-important factor, rather than the appearance of the aquarium, can use an inside type as long as it is capable of doing the job.

Think about investing in a power filter, ie a type that has an increased water flow rate because it uses an electric pump rather than an air-lift to move the water. The returning clean water from such filters can be redistributed across the aquarium by means of a spray bar, which also serves to reduce the pressure of the returning water quite considerably.

There is always a possibility that

Left and below: *Modern internal filters can fit unobtrusively into the corner of even the simplest aquarium set-up. These latest models have the advantage of two-stage filtration with the sponge and a separate filter media container (see explanatory cutaway, left). Additional aeration for the aquarium can also be provided via the venturi.*

fishes will uncover a biological filter system's plates or tubes while foraging in the gravel. This can be prevented by placing a protective mesh above the first 2.5cm (1in) of gravel before adding the rest to complete the aquarium floor furnishing.

The water flow through a biological filtration system can be increased in one of two ways: a motorized impeller can be fitted to the uplift tube (in a down-flow system), or an external power filter can be connected to the input tube (in an up-flow system). It is usual to supplement biological filtration in coldwater aquariums by some form of mechanical filtration, to help clear the water of suspended matter. Many fishkeepers advocate using a reverse-flow biologcal filter (passing water up through the gravel) so that suspended matter is not drawn down into the gravel but captured by the mechanical filter on its way to the biological filter.

Below: *Modern self-priming external canister filters are ideal because of their ease of storage.*

Lighting

Lighting plays a very important role in the healthy functioning of the aquarium, in addition to letting the fishkeeper see his collection of fishes.

Light provides stimulus for activity and growth, and enables the aquarium plants to perform their most important function, photosynthesis. This is absolutely vital to the healthy condition of the aquarium and is further discussed in the section on plants, pages 28-31.

The light for any aquarium comes ideally from directly overhead, although a little sidelighting in the form of daylight through the front glass is quite permissible (see the section on tank location, page 15) and may well highlight some of those wonderful iridescences in the fishes' scales. The amount of light falling on or into the aquarium is also critical, contributing directly to the health of the aquarium.

Lighting takes two forms: tungsten or fluorescent. The relative advantages and disadvantages can be considered by reference to the accompanying table.

The quantity of light is fairly critical. Too little light will result in the growth of brown algae and the plants will not flourish; too much light will result in the growth of green algae and the plants will be smothered. As a starting guide, allow 40 watts of tungsten light and 10 watts of fluorescent light for every $900cm^2$ ($1ft^2$) of water surface area. It may be necessary to increase these figures, if a tank deeper than 38cm (15in) is used. There is no objection to mixing the two types of lighting in order to provide the type of lighting that you prefer. The aquarium should be lit for between 10 and 15 hours each day; the final figure is best found by trial and error.

Light should be used as efficiently as possible. The reflector/hood fitting should be painted white inside or lined with metal foil (a roll of cooking foil is a good source!) and it should be designed so that the light is reflected down and backwards into the tank to avoid casting disturbing shadows towards the viewer.

Protect your lamps from condensation damage and water splashes by using waterproof lampholders and a cover glass between the reflector and the water surface. Cover glasses also keep dust out of the aquarium, stop fishes leaping out, keep plants from being scorched by the heat of tungsten lamps and cut down evaporation losses. Keep them scrupulously clean so that the amount of light reaching the aquarium from the lamps is not reduced.

Below: *This table compares the advantages and disadvantages of tungsten and fluorescent lighting.*

TUNGSTEN	FLUORESCENT
Inexpensive and simple to install	Expensive and more complicated to install
Short lamp life	Long lamp life
High running costs	Low running costs
May overheat surface layers of the water	Cool running
Only one choice of 'colour' available with 'clear' or 'pearl' glass bulbs	Various 'colours' available to enhance fish colours or to promote plant growth
Easy to regulate	Difficult to regulate
Various wattages (brightness) available	Uniform strength of light only (approximately 10 watts per 30cm/12in length)

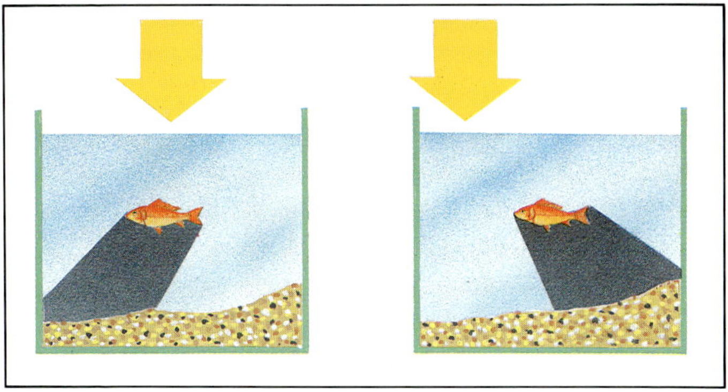

Above: *The appearance of the fishes in the aquarium depends to a great extent on how they are lit – both with the type of light and the positioning of it. A lamp placed centrally (left) will cast a shadow toward the viewer; a lamp placed toward the front will not (right), allowing the fishes to be seen clearly without shadows.*

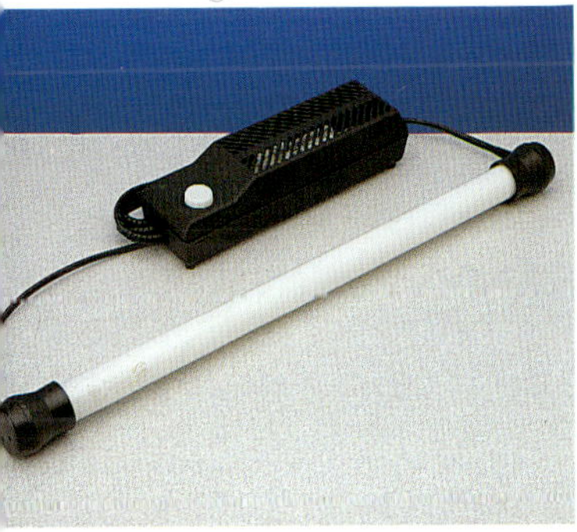

Left: *A modern convertagear with a high specification tube designed to promote aquatic plant growth. Fluorescents like this need the convertagear unit in order to illuminate the tube.*

Below: *The importance of fluorescent tubes to modern tank set-ups means that hoods very often come provided with clips to hold the fluorescent tubes and a space at the rear to house the convertagear.*

Water requirements

It would be wrong to assume that because coldwater fishes need none of the elaborate technical equipment to stabilize their water temperature, they can be kept in any type of water. Fishes of any species depend on the quality of water for their very livelihood and the fishkeeper should be aware of this from the outset.

Despite the abundance of water on the face of the earth, only a small proportion of it is inhabited by freshwater fishes, and these species also live in differing locations and water conditions. How does the fishkeeper cope successfully with all these variables?

Water quality

Fortunately, coldwater fishes are less susceptible to changes in their water conditions than some tropical fishes. They can cope quite happily with the changing temperatures through the seasons of the year in an outside pond, and are quite at home in the fishkeeper-controlled environment of the indoor aquarium.

It is true to say that most of the water used for fishkeeping, in aquarium or pond, comes from the domestic household supply, and this is usually quite suitable. Domestic water is provided as fit for human consumption, and fortunately we do not have to re-treat it for fishkeeping use, although there are one or two precautions that we should take.

Below: *The quality of water can be changed at any time, from its origin as rain to the time it reaches the sea again, or even in your aquarium.*

The main small cause for concern is the chlorine content, but vigorous aeration will soon drive out this gas; alternatively, water from the tap can be left to stand for a few days until the chlorine has dissipated itself naturally; or dechlorinating products (available from your aquatic dealer) can be used to nullify the effect of chlorine.

Another danger is from toxic metals in the water, such as zinc or copper; this can occur where water has stood for long periods before use in a brand new plumbing system. The remedy here is to run this standing water to waste rather than use it in the aquarium. Again, proprietary treatments will precipitate these metals, rendering the water safe.

Water conditions in an outdoor pond will be affected by rainfall, by leaves falling in the pond, and sometimes by such occurrences as the influx of chemicals from garden sprays and insecticides. It should be unnecessary to warn against using metal fixtures or accessories in either pond or aquarium.

Water hardness and pH

Goldfishes and other coldwater fishes will tolerate a wide range of water conditions, and here we are referring to the water's qualities of hardness and acidity or alkalinity. Water is hard or soft depending on the amount of salts (usually of calcium and magnesium) dissolved in it. Water from chalky soil is hard, whereas water from a moorland stream is generally soft. Water hardness is measured in degrees and usually quoted as °DH, °GH or °KH. °DH and

The nitrogen cycle

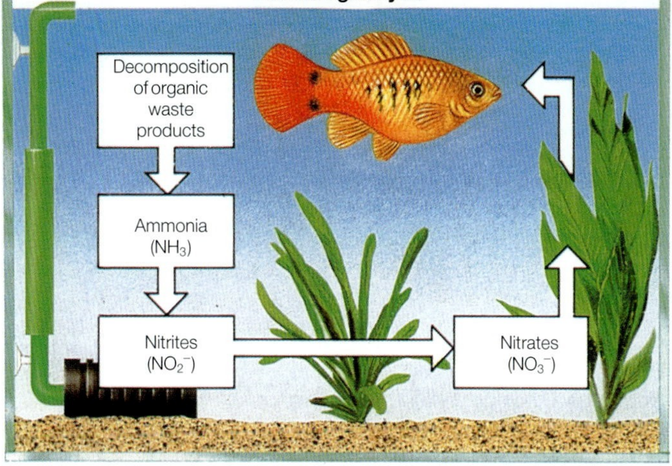

°GH are usually measures of total hardness, but °KH measures hardness due solely to carbonates. The difference in the figures will represent hardness due to non-carbonates.

The acidity or alkalinity of water is affected by gases absorbed from the atmosphere as it falls as rain, and by minerals and other substances that dissolve into it during its passage through and over the ground en route back to the sea. Acidity or alkalinity is measured logarithmically on a scale known as the pH scale. This ranges from 0 to 14 (strongest acid to strongest alkali) but the range that is of concern to fishkeepers lies in a very narrow band, approximately pH 6.5-8.0, which is slightly acid to slightly alkaline. The effect of variations of pH on a fish, such as a Goldfish, is improved colours in acidic water and an increase in the mucus covering of ths fish's body in alkaline water conditions.

Kits are available to test water hardness, pH and nitrite content, if the fishkeeper becomes particularly interested in this aspect of the hobby, although it is not strictly necessary to do so, and many fishkeepers are not so scientifically interested. However, it may become necessary to keep a check on the water's qualities when breeding, in order to keep a detailed record of the conditions that produce optimum results.

Above: *The nitrogen cycle shows how organic nitrogen is circulated in the aquatic environment. Plants are eaten by fish which then excrete toxic ammonia which is broken down by* nitrosomonus *bacteria into nitrite. This nitrite is then broken down by* nitrobacter *bacteria into the less harmful nitrate which is then used by the plants. And so the cycle continues.*

The main thing is to be aware of such qualities of water, so that you can understand how changing them can have repercussions on your fish's wellbeing in pond or aquarium.

Maintaining stable conditions

Fishes should not be subjected to sudden changes in their water conditions or temperature; when transferring a fish from one location to another, care should be taken to make the changeover as smooth as possible. This means equalizing the temperatures of the two bodies of water, and trying to ensure that the water qualities are approximately the same. Fishes suddenly exposed to different conditions will become stressed, and while stressed may contract an ailment to which they were previously immune.

Aquarium plants

There are a number of plants suitable for the coldwater aquarium, although by no means such a varied selection as is usually available for the tropical aquarium.

The value of plants

Aquarium plants serve several purposes. They provide shelter, food and spawning site materials for the fishes, and they also beautify the aquarium for the benefit of the fishkeeper. But their most important function of all is to help maintain the aquarium in good condition.

Under the action of daylight or an illuminated aquarium, plants store food in their green cells by a process called photosynthesis. During this process carbon dioxide is used and oxygen is given off by the plant. Here is a perfectly natural way of reducing the level of carbon dioxide in the aquarium, in addition to the help given by aeration. This beneficial action occurs only when the aquarium is illuminated; during periods of darkness the plants consume oxygen and give off carbon dioxide themselves, just as the fishes do for 24 hours a day. For this reason, levels of carbon dioxide may build up during the night in densely planted and heavily populated tanks.

Above: *The plants' beneficial action of absorbing carbon dioxide during daylight ceases at night, and they use up oxygen just like the fishes.*

Below: *In addition to looking decorative, plants can be vital in the aquarium to ensure its continuing health and success.*

Above: Myriophyllum spicatum *is a fine-leaved plant ideally suited to creating a bushy effect. It needs clean water conditions to thrive.*

Above: *Note how the reddish tinge of* Ceratophyllum submersum *(centre) blends in well with the piece of petrified wood in this aquarium.*

Selecting aquarium plants

The selection of plants is not critical, but some thought has to be given to those species used in the coldwater aquarium. The soft-leaved varieties are likely to be nibbled by the fishes. Fortunately, soft leaved plants are often fast growers, and losses can soon be made good.

When planting the aquarium, the fishkeeper has two aims: to make the aquarium look nice, and to disguise the fact that it is really nothing more than a glass box filled with water. Plants should be arranged in clumps, not in regimented rows, and their crowns (the junction between stem and root system at gravel level) should be protected with small pebbles to prevent uprooting by the fishes as they search for food.

Tall, strap-like plants such as *Sagittaria* and *Vallisneria* are useful as concealing plants for the side and rear walls of the aquarium. There are several varieties of these plants, some with broad leaves, others with tightly twisted leaves. Propagation is by runners from the parent plant, and the young ones can easily be carefully disconnected and planted elsewhere in the aquarium.

The rather fleshy leaves of *Ludwigia,* emerging from opposite sides of a central stem, are pale green with, in some species, a pink-red underside. Several species within this genus are suitable for the coldwater aquarium, and they make very attractive clumps. Cuttings taken from this plant will root when replanted in the gravel. A similar one is *Bacopa caroliniana,* a bog plant that may take on a reddish tinge.

Below: Egeria densa, *a fast-growing plant that can be easily propagated by taking cuttings. These soon re-root to form healthy new plants.*

With these species that are naturally used to growing emerse (out of water) for some periods of the year, it may be worth growing some plants in this way before transferring them to the aquarium in order to produce a continuity of submerged stock.

Acorus and *Eleocharis* are used to cover the gravel. *Acorus gramineus* is a small submerged rush and propagation is by division of the rhizome or rootstock. *Eleocharis acicularis* has the very apt common name of Hairgrass, and one look at its straight needle-like leaves will reveal why. It is often featured placed in front of large rocks, which seem to set off its appearance very well. Propagation is by runners, and dividing a clump will often encourage new growth.

Bushy species such as *Myriophyllum* and *Lagarosiphon* help to fill spaces quickly; but they need a strong light, so watch out for growths of algae, which will choke the fine leaves. They are also liable to become choked in dirty water conditions. Another favourite aquarium plant, particularly in tropical aquariums, is *Cabomba,* and it may be possible to acquire species of this fine-leaved genus that can acclimatize to cooler conditions. Propagate these genera by cuttings; these may be weighted down with thin strips of lead until re-rooting occurs.

Certain aquarium plants feed through their leaves and do not depend on their roots for absorbing nourishment; they may not actually anchor themselves in the gravel at all but simply float around in midwater as a somewhat tangled mass. Hornwort *(Ceratophyllum demersum)* and Canadian Pondweed *(Elodea canadensis)* are typical examples. Make sure that the plants you choose are suitable for the coldwater aquarium; some varieties have become acclimatized to growing in the tropical aquarium and will not withstand the transfer back to lower temperatures. These fast-growing species will provide an abundance of

Vallisneria is ideal for background filling.

Ludwigia looks well as a contrasting leaf form.

Short-growing Acorus is a good foreground aquarium plant.

Aquarium plants
Using aquarium plants well involves careful choice and positioning. Protect their crowns with pebbles.

cuttings from which new stock can be grown for further tanks.

Floating plants bring shade to the aquarium and provide a safe refuge for young fishes. *Lemna minor* (Duckweed) spreads so quickly that the fishkeeper often regrets introducing it in the first place! Apart from this nuisance value, duckweed will also keep out a lot of the light meant for other plants in the aquarium. *Riccia fluitans* (Crystalwort) is much more decorative and hangs just below the surface; it is an ideal spawning medium and a hiding place for fry. It is not frost hardy. *Azolla caroliniana* (Fairy Moss) is a colourful floating plant with proportionately long trailing roots. The leaves have a velvety appearance, and air trapped in the hairs on the leaves' surface soon rights the plant if it is placed in the water upside down.

An underwater plant from the fern family is *Fontinalis antipyretica* (Willow Moss). This clings to the surface of a submerged log or stone and is highly decorative as well as being an ideal spawning medium. It may become clogged with suspended material, but it can be removed from the tank, still attached to its stone, and given a good rinse under a running tap to clear off the detritus – another good reason for having an efficient filtration system fitted in the aquarium.

The question will arise whether or not to use plants collected from a local stream or river in the aquarium. Obviously, costs are small and stocks can be easily replaced; but there is a danger of introducing into the aquarium not only disease, but also snails' eggs and the larvae of predacious insects that will attack young fishes. All plants should be thoroughly inspected before introducing them into the aquarium, and a rinse in a weak solution of potassium permanganate will also help to destroy any unwanted 'passengers' on the leaves of the plants – especially important if they are collected from the wild.

Azolla is a delicate floating plant ideal for bringing shade to the aquarium.

Myriophyllum fills the corners. When pruned, the plant tends to become even bushier still.

Specimen plants can be planted in nutrient-enriched soil in pots buried in the gravel.

Setting up the tank

The initial setting up of an aquarium should be an enjoyable experience, culminating in a fully furnished aquarium ready to receive the fishes. The path to achieving this end result can be difficult and messy or relatively easy and well ordered, depending on the preparatory work carried out beforehand.

It is as well to have everything you will need ready to hand, including pliers, screwdrivers, a sharp knife and a sense of humour. The actual site of the aquarium and surrounding area should be kept clear of tools, equipment and onlookers, but you should have a table within easy reach on which can be laid out the 'ingredients' for the tank – rocks, plants, filters, etc. Some of the furnishings can be installed in the tank prior to placing it in its final position, although this is only possible with tanks up to 60cm (24in) in length; above this size, furnish the tank *in situ* or have a helping hand to carry the tank into position. Remember to place that slab of expanded polystyrene in position first – it's a terrible thing to remember it only when you have finished the whole job!

Filters and gravel

If you are using biological filtration, the filter plate must go into the tank before anything else. Make sure it covers the entire tank base and it is quite level all round the edges. The air-lift pipe should be fitted before any gravel is added. Stand large rocks or logs cemented to their base plates on the first layer of gravel over the filter plate, on top of the protective nylon mesh, to prevent them from toppling over if the fishes dig too deeply in the gravel later on. Alternatively, they can be placed directly on the tank base if no undergravel biological filter is used.

Gravel goes in next and should be of sufficient depth to allow the plants to root satisfactorily and to ensure that an undergravel filter (if fitted) will operate correctly. A layer of at least 5-7.5cm (2-3in) is necessary, and this

Left: *Carefully add the substrate by the handful or use a plastic measuring jug, taking care not to drop the gravel from a height. Although sold as 'washed', aquarium sand and gravel still contain dust that you must first flush away.*

Right: *Position the return jet of an external power filter in the rear corner, so that the flow is just below the water surface. Fix it to the outside glass with suckers. Position the intake assembly in the other rear corner, with the strainer basket just above the substrate surface.*

may be increased so that the gravel bed can be landscaped to give a more pleasing underwater picture. Small rocks or pieces of slate can be embedded in the gravel to form terraces, which help to give a sense of depth to the tank.

Filtration equipment is fitted before the final rockwork or other decorations; this is partly for ease of fitting and partly so that you can use the decorations to hide the hardware. If you use an external power filter - ideal for messy coldwater fishes - the intake and return pipes can be hidden like this.

Adding the plants

Before planting, fill the tank with water to within 7.5-10cm (3-4in) of the top of the tank. This empty space will allow for any displacement of water by your arms when planting, and the tank will not overflow. Take care, when filling, that the carefully contoured gravel is not flattened by the force of water coming from the hosepipe; a small jug or deep saucer placed on the gravel will dissipate the water pressure. Another reason for planting the tank with water in it, is that the plants immediately take up their natural positions and the effects of planting can be evaluated.

The plants should be within easy reach while you plant the aquarium. It is a good idea to sort them out into species groups and forms – i.e. tall plants, bushy types, foreground species – ahead of planting time. They can be kept moist by putting them between layers of very wet newspaper until required.

It is usually best to plant from round the edges and back of the tank inwards, ending up with the foreground and specimen plants. Clumps of tall plants can be used to hide the side walls and rear of the tank, with bushy types filling the corners and in front of any hardware. Make sure that all the plant roots are slightly trimmed. Also consider using plastic plants, which are ideal for tanks with boisterous fishes.

Left: *With the heater installed (needed for some 'coldwater' fishes) and rocks in place,start by adding water from a clean jug onto a saucer. This avoids disturbing the prewashed substrate. Fill the tank to 10cm (4in) below the final water level.*

Right: *It is best to plant your tank before it is fully topped up, otherwise your hand and arm will displace water, causing it to spill out of the tank. Fine-leaved plastic plants trap masses of tiny air bubbles when they are first put into the tank, but they will disappear in a day or two.*

back to encourage the growth of new roots. Spread the roots out in the gravel and remember not to bury the crown of the plant in the gravel, or the plant will rot away in a short time. The best way to do this, is deliberately to put the plant in too deeply, and then gently pull it up to its correct position. Specimen plants should be planted in pre-formed, nutritious 'plant plugs', which are then buried in the gravel. Alternatively, such species can be cultivated in shallow pots, which are then buried. A layer of small pebbles around the plant crowns will prevent uprooting. After planting, the tank should be filled completely.

Air pump and lighting
The air pump should be installed ideally above the water level, but if precautions are taken to prevent back-siphoning it can be situated on a convenient shelf below the tank. The air valves are stuck to the aquarium side and the air supply tubing connected (do not forget the check valve) from the pump's outlet and to the filters and/or airstones.

A 'cable tidy' will make the electrical connections neater and safer, and provide convenient switching circuits for the pump and lights, but the pump should not be switched off if it is supplying air to a biological filter.

Cover glasses are fitted by means of special supporting clips (avoid metal ones) or simply by resting on a narrow glass shelf built into the all-glass tank. A corner of the cover glass can be cut off to allow the insertion of airlines, and maybe a small aperture cut at the front for ease of access while feeding.

The reflector/hood should present no problems, but if it contains the necessary starter equipment for fluorescent lighting, be careful when placing it on the tank, as it will be extra heavy and may break the cover glass. If tungsten lamps are to be used, ensure that sufficient ventilation holes exist in the hood, to prevent the build-up of heat, which will affect the top water layers and also shorten the lamps' life.

Although a coldwater aquarium does not generally have live electrical equipment in the water, as does the tropical aquarium, it is nevertheless good (and safe) practice always to disconnect the electricity supply from any piece of equipment while carrying out necessary maintenance or any adjustment it may need.

Planting the aquarium
Plant the aquarium with a purpose; it should look natural, not formal, but avoid making it look untidy.

Fill the tank completely when planting is finished.

Hide any unsightly filter pipes and siphon tubes behind bushy plants.

Bury 'plant plugs' in the gravel bed.

Final checks
The operation of the filter and aeration can now be checked and adjusted by means of the air valves; power filters need to be primed with water before the final return hose connections are made. Make sure that all water-carrying hose connections are secure; even a small amount of spilt water makes a mess, so you can imagine what damage the contents of a 68 litre (15 gallon) tank could do. Any scum on the water surface (dust from the gravel) can be removed with a sheet of absorbent paper drawn across the surface.

The tank is now ready for the fishes, although some fishkeepers give time for the tank to settle down and the plants to take root. The biological filter will take a period of time to develop a mature colony of bacteria and this

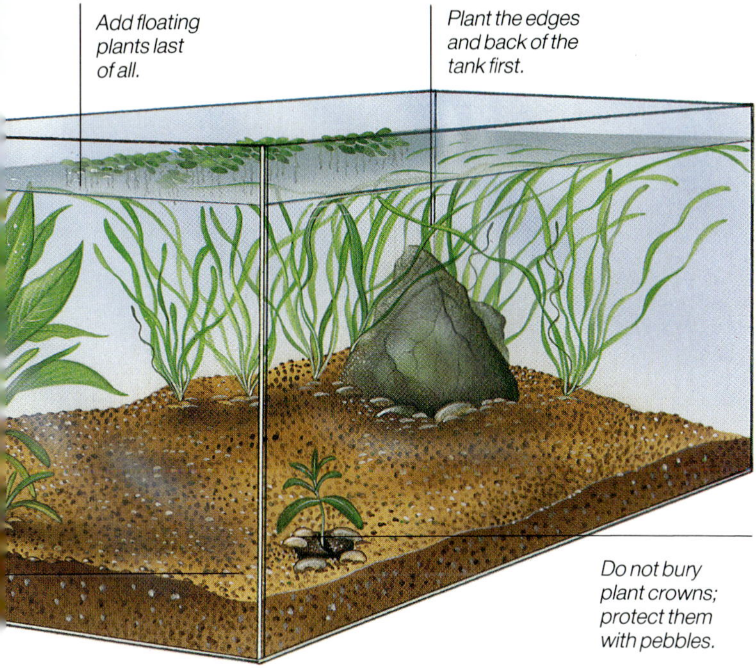

can be hastened by adding either some gravel from an established aquarium or one or two hardy fishes to provide the initial ammonia and waste products for the bacteria to work on and multiply.

Below: *A piece of driftwood has been used well here to add perspective to the tank and to disguise its box shape. Note that the aquarium plants are growing in separate species clumps, not all mixed up together.*

Ponds

The magic sound of the movement of water, the lazy rise of a fish and the beauty of the water lily all conjure up visions of idyllic summer evenings by the water. The temptation to add a pond to the garden must be very great if you are any sort of fishkeeper.

Just as we considered the basic sizes and locations for the indoor aquarium, so must we do the same for the outdoor pond. The site, shape, size and method of construction of the pond must be decided in the light of various factors before any actual installation begins.

What size of pond?

The size of the pond must suit its surroundings (even if the keen fishkeeper secretly wants 'wall-to-wall water'). Too large a pond would dominate the garden, and would be a chilling outlook during winter.

Choosing above a minimum size of pond will, in a similar way to the considerations for the indoor aquarium, lead towards stable water conditions. A water surface area of something in excess of 4.5m^2 (approximately 50ft^2) is a good guide. This sounds large, but when drawn out to scale on paper it will not seem over-ambitious; a pond 3×1.5m (10×5ft) or 2.4m (8ft) square, or a circular pond of 2.4m (8ft) diameter, suddenly all become quite feasible.

The other dimension of the pond, its depth, must also be considered. Goldfishes can perhaps tolerate a minimum depth of about 75cm (30in) during winter months, but if Koi are to be kept a more practical and safe depth would be something approaching 1.5m (5ft). The latter depth will enable the fishes to overwinter safely under any ice .hat forms on the pond.

Pond location

Where should a pond be situated? It would be nice to see it from the house, but not immediately outside the windows. Underneath trees is NOT a good place for several reasons. Ponds are often sited beneath trees on the assumption that direct sunlight will be bad for it, and the shade afforded by the trees will alleviate this problem: this doubtful 'advantage' is far outweighed by the drawbacks to such a siting. Leaves, fruit, sap, bird-droppings, etc. will all fall into the pond, with subsequent deterioration of the water conditions; some tree leaves and flowers are indeed poisonous. And tree roots may puncture a pond liner.

The pond should have access to it (for viewing the fish and plants, and for maintenance); any nearby footpath can be utilized. Similarly, necessary services such as water and electricity should be either within reach or easily installed.

The best situation for the pond is out in the open where it can receive at least five hours of direct sunshine each day. It can of course be situated near a sheltering hedge or fence to keep off strong prevailing winds. The problem of too much direct sunshine can be overcome by the judicious planting of sufficient number of water lilies to cover perhaps two thirds of the water surface. In this way, there will be confidence-giving shade for

Below: *A cross-section of a typical pond showing the basic design features involved. These apply to ponds of all construction types.*

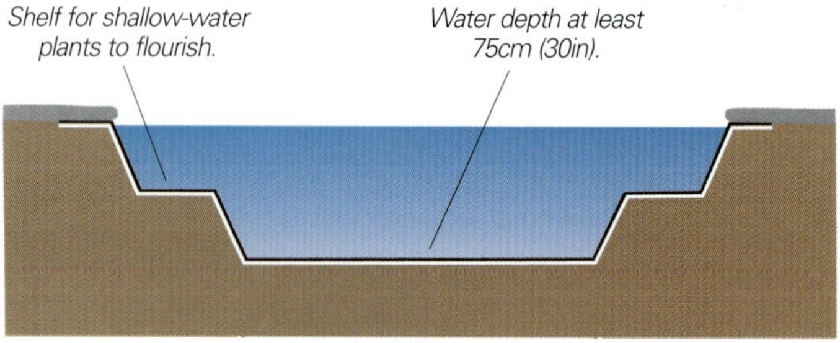

Above: *Choosing the best position for the pond. Keep it away from tree roots and falling leaves, clear of the house but sheltered from prevailing winds. Direct sunshine will not harm it; shade can be provided by the leaves of water lilies growing across the surface. Provide easy viewing access.*

Above: *This informal pond has an interesting shape, with a correct proportion of water lilies and marginal plants. Note that it is in the open, away from overhanging trees.*

Above: *Patio pools should not be too small if sufficient space is available. This design of pool is excellent; it is not too predictable and even sports a modest fountain for added style.*

the fishes, protection from predators and enough competiton from the plants to crowd out unwanted green algae that may develop.

Pond design

Style is also important, in order for the pond to harmonize with the rest of the garden. Straight paths and clipped hedges demand a formal pond of precise design (rectangular or square); a more natural-looking aspect will go better with an informal pond of irregular shape sunk into the ground, with perhaps a neighbouring rockery or bank.

Patio ponds are usually not successful, as they are of necessity small, and well under our self-imposed minimum dimensions. On the other hand, a raised brick-built patio pond of sufficient size can provide a very striking feature, especially when floodlit.

Pond construction

The pond's construction can be of three types: concrete, pre-formed or liner. Of these, the first is the most labour-intensive but probably the most permanent. The two other types require the excavation of the hole in an identical way, but from then on the rest is much easier.

Pre-formed ponds come with built-in ledges (for the marginal plants and shallow-water-loving species) already incorporated in their design, whereas the liner pond must have the ledges left when the excavation is carried out.

The design of pre-formed ponds often verges on the fanciful, with exaggerated 'kidney shapes' that, in practical terms, never look quite the same in the ground with a surround covering the edges. Remember that the pond is usually seen from close to, not from high above. A further criticism of these ponds is that they are usually not deep enough, although recent designs seem to be correcting this deficiency.

Liner ponds may be of plastic, laminated PVC, or butyl rubber; these are in ascending order of cost, and with increasing longevity. For the fishkeeper who wants to tailor his pond to his own requirements, the liner pond is the most popular method using modern materials and technology.

When calculating the size of liner necessary for the excavated hole, a reasonable guide is to add twice the depth measurement to length and width dimensions. This will give enough for an adequate turned-over top edge, to be covered by paving stones that will hide it.

Below: *Pond shells are made in a range of plastics – the most rigid being reinforced with fibreglass. When buying a shell, check for holes and cracks. If water gets in and freezes, the shell will split.*

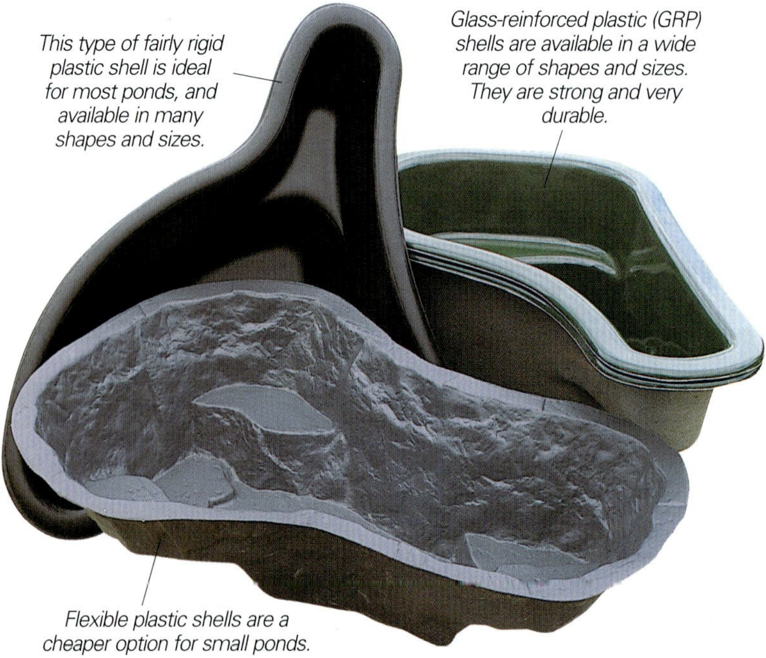

This type of fairly rigid plastic shell is ideal for most ponds, and available in many shapes and sizes.

Glass-reinforced plastic (GRP) shells are available in a wide range of shapes and sizes. They are strong and very durable.

Flexible plastic shells are a cheaper option for small ponds.

Left: *To install a liner pond, mark out the shape, construct a concrete collar, then mark out the shelves. Remove the topsoil and keep it for later. Dig out the rest of the pond, sloping the sides. Make the base as flat as possible.*

Left: *Remove sharp stones and line the pond first with spun underlay and then a good-quality liner. Push it into shape and add some water. Trim off the excess liner so that the remaining liner covers half the collar. If in doubt, cut too little off the first time.*

Left: *Cut paving to size, lay a deep bed of mortar and twist the paving into place, level, and tamp with a hammer handle.*

Below: *Install the waterfall, rockery and filter system before planting up the finished pond.*

Pond plants

Whereas the plants in an indoor aquarium cannot range beyond their container, the outdoor pond can 'spread' beyond its confines and apparently progress from purely aquatic plants to terrestrial species, by way of the marginal species around its edges. This feature completes the integration of the pond into the garden layout in the most natural way possible.

Not all pond plants can be planted in the gravel at the bottom of the pond; many require shallow water conditions and are grown in ledges around the edge, or in baskets supported on a brick plinth in the main body of water. Other species grow free-floating with no permanent anchorage.

Before the various species of plants are described, the question of the planting medium must be settled. It is not necessary to cover the pond floor with a deep layer of soil in order to grow aquatic plants; it is true that this will produce rampant growth, but it will also result in rather cloudy water, preventing the fishkeeper seeing the fishes. Plants, especially water lilies, are best grown in pots so that their cultivation can be more easily controlled. It also means that there is less mess to contend with when clearing out the pond.

A deep layer of gravel will be necessary if the pond is to be filtered by a biological (undergravel) filter system, although there is no reason why the gravel filter medium cannot be kept in a box outside the pond and fed via the submersible pump as before. If an undergravel filter system is incorporated in the pond, the excavated depth should be increased to accommodate the deep layer of gravel necessary to form the filter bed in which the bacteria live.

The water plants are best divided into four groups: submerged plants, rooting plants with surface leaves and/or flowers, floating plants and marginals.

Submerged plants
Into this group come the 'oxygenators', although their value is probably more as carbon dioxide consumers and as spawning media. These plants grow satisfactorily in gravel and can be bunched together (in genus groups) and rooted in containers of gravel; plastic seed trays about 5cm (2in) deep are ideal because they accommodate a fair number of plants, making it unnecessary to cover the pond floor in plant pots. Oxygenators feed through their leaves and need their roots for anchorage only, so planting them in trays will not prevent them from feeding correctly.

Callitriche (Starwort) is a fast grower with narrow leaves. Some fishes will browse on it.

Ceratophyllum demersum (Hornwort) is a brittle mass of spiky whorls. It may die back in winter. This species is free-floating, and hardly ever roots.

Egeria densa, also known as *Elodea densa,* has narrow tightly curled leaves. It will grow very long and can be propagated by cuttings.

Fontinalis antipyretica (Willow moss) is a plant that attaches itself to surfaces, and it should be transferred intact with its site. Propagate by careful division.

Below: *Marginal plants occupy the shelf around the pond; other plants, such as water lilies, are grown in pots on the pond bottom or on brick plinths, depending on the depth.*

Largarosiphon major, also known as *Elodea crispa,* is similar to *E. densa,* but it may not survive frost.

Above left: Fontinalis antipyretica *(Willow Moss), an excellent spawning medium.* Right: Lagarosiphon major.

Myriophyllum sp. (Water milfoils, Featherfoils) are excellent spawning media, but they need clean water and plenty of light. *M. verticillatum* and *M. spicatum* prefer acid and alkaline water respectively.

Najas species all have a mass of narrow leaves.

Potamogeton (Pondweed). *P. crispus* and *P. densus* are more suitable than *P. natans*, which grows very rampant.

Sagittaria has several forms, which produce totally submerged, surface or aerial leaves, or combinations of all three. Some are more suitable for the indoor aquarium than for the outdoor pond. Check your local supplier.

Utricularia vulgaris (Bladderwort) is a floating (submerged) species that has tiny bladders in which small crustaceans may be trapped.

Floating plants
Some of the floating species described in the previous section on plants for the aquarium may be transferred to the outdoor pond not only with some success, but very often with too much success. *Azolla* and *Lemna* will take over the entire water surface and prove difficult enough to control in a small pond, let alone in a large one. Other species will not survive low temperatures. On balance, it is probably best to leave the responsibility of covering the pond surface from sunshine to more decorative species of rooted plants, whose leaves do the job better and without disastrous results.

Rooted species with floating leaves
Top of this list must come the Water Lily (*Nymphaea*), the plant that everyone associates with the garden pond, and this section will be restricted to this attractive species.

There are many hardy varieties of water lily, thanks to the Frenchman Latour-Marliac, whose work on hybridization has enabled future generations to cultivate this beautiful plant in climates cooler than the plant's original home.

The water lily needs to be planted at various depths according to the variety. This is easily achieved by varying the height of its pot on a pile of

Right: Nymphaea *'Rose Arey', a superb water lily for small ponds. Needs a water depth of 45cm (18in).*

Far right: Nymphaea *'James Brydon'. This prolific hybrid will tolerate more shade than most water lilies. For small and medium-sized ponds.*

Below: Nymphaea *'Candida'. This is one of the pygmy water lilies that will thrive in water only 23cm (9in) deep. Lovely cup-shaped flowers.*

Below: Nymphaea marliacea chromatella. *A justifiably popular hybrid with flowers up to 18cm (7in) across. Excellent for larger ponds.*

bricks within the pond. Planting should be in soil, topped off with a layer of gravel and a few pebbles to discourage foraging fishes. The tip of the rhizome/tuberous root should be left showing a little. Place the pot in about 20-30cm (8-12in) of water until the leaves start to appear, then move the plant to its correct (depth) position in the pond. The best time to transfer water lilies is in late spring, before the vigorous growth begins; growth would otherwise be checked by the plant's move later in the season.

Below: *The straight edges of this formal pond have been softened by the clever use of marginal plants.*

Marginal plants

These plants are grown in the shallow ledges around the pond. The ledges are moulded into the design of pre-formed ponds, or left unexcavated during the construction of lined or concrete ponds.

The marginals used should be in scale with the size of the pond. Many small ponds have been lost to view behind a massive clump of irises, due to careless choice of species. Marginals also look better in species clumps, not all mixed up together. The following genera are suitable and will provide a good selection. *Acorus, Alisma, Calla, Caltha, Iris, Lobelia, Ranunculus, Typha.*

Filters and fountains

The clarity of pond water can be maintained by the use of a filter system. This can be a box containing a filter medium, such as Alfagrog (ceramic rock) or biomedia, through which the pond water is passed. Water movement is achieved by means of an electrically driven water pump. The pump may be of a submersible or a non-submersible design, depending on your needs.

The pond filter

The filter is fed via the pond pump and will both mechanically clean and biologically filter the water. The bacteria that grow in the filter media process the waste produced by the fish, which if left untreated would poison the fish. These bacteria require a constant flow of oxygenated water to survive.

Always follow the manufacturer's guidelines on water volume and stocking levels when selecting a filter for your pond.

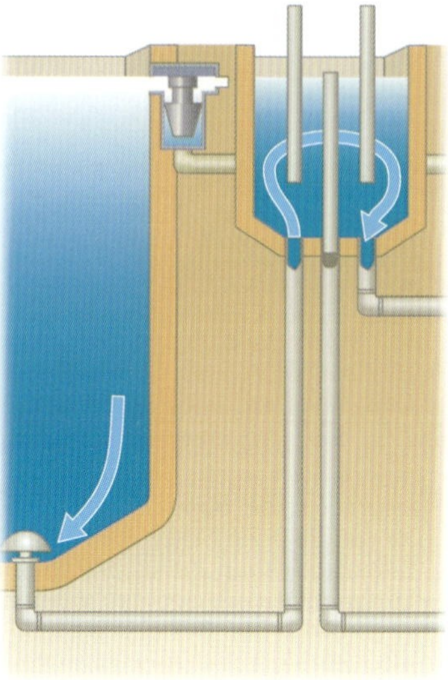

Above: *This drain system for koi ponds must be incorporated when building the pond; it cannot be added later. The drain can be either connected to a sewer or, more commonly, fed directly into the filtration system of the pond. When the standpipe is removed or the valve is opened, the difference in water level causes the flow of water.*

A box filter

Connect the filter inlet to the pump, which should have the capacity to pass around 50 litres (11 gallons) per hour, for larger ponds this rate should be increased. (This water flow rate is for biological filtration purposes and is not a figure for other water movements such as fountains or complex waterfalls.) The return from whatever filter system is used can conveniently be directed back into the pond by way of a small cascade; this will also increase the aeration of the water.

Ponds containing Koi are often fitted with a special type of filtration system designed to work siphonically rather than by mechanical means. This system has to be incorporated into the pond's original construction and cannot be added later.

Water pumps

Pumps are often required to provide decorative water movements, as a fountain, waterfall or system of cascades. In this instance, careful selection is needed to find the most suitable-sized pump. Fountains require a pump with plenty of pressure, whereas waterfalls and complex cascades need a pump with sufficient volume-carrying capacity.

Fountains are generally associated with large formal ponds where there is ample room for their falling spray to avoid the water lilies, which do not take kindly to being permanently waterlogged.

Waterfalls and cascades are usually designed to be incorporated into a pondside rockery. The choice of a pump of the correct power is vital, particularly if the water has to be raised any appreciable height above the pond level.

Many pond plants dislike water currents, and the problem of excessive water movement through the pond can be solved by drawing the input to the pump from as near to the return to the pond as possible. In this instance, the pump is acting only as a mover of water, and it will not be any good incorporating a filter system in the water circuit (except a strainer to safeguard the pump from clogging up), as very little water will be drawn from other parts of the pond.

In order for the pump to operate at full efficiency, the input pipe from the pond should be as short as possible, and of non-collapsible construction. Non-submersible pumps should be kept in a weatherproof but well-ventilated box. The electrical fittings should also be well protected.

Below: *Submersible pond pumps, such as this robust amphibious style pump, can be used either in or out of water. Choose a pump and filter with the correct flow rate and capacity for your pond.*

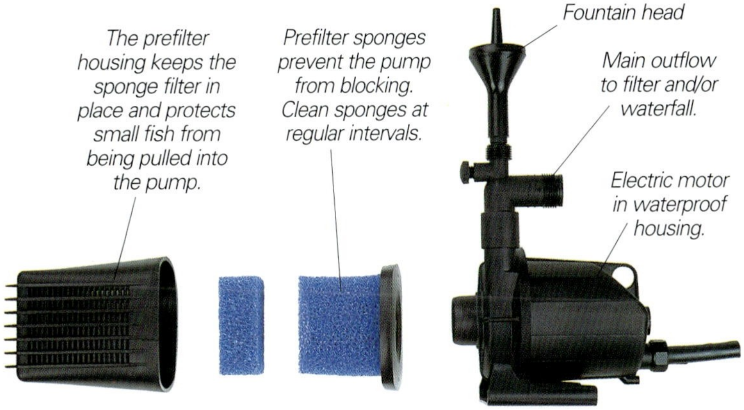

Feeding

There is a difference between the feeding of aquarium fishes and pond fishes. Fishes kept in an indoor aquarium are used to fairly stable environmental conditions, with relatively small changes in water temperature, and a regular supply of food by courtesy of the fishkeeper. Aquarium fishes will therefore feed (and need to be fed) all the year round.

Pond fishes are affected much more by the changing temperatures of the seasons and the varying supply of natural foods occurring in the pond. As temperatures fall during autumn, the supply of food diminishes. With the onset of winter and temperatures below 4°C (40°F), the fish's metabolism slows down and the fish enters a state of almost total hibernation, during which time it needs no food; it regains its appetite only as water temperatures rise again in the spring.

Fishes in a new pond require feeding by the fishkeeper until the pond can provide almost all the fishes' needs. It is also recommended that pond fishes are given extra food as autumn approaches (their appetite increases at this time too), so that they can build up enough physical reserves to see them through the winter months.

The Goldfish, and most coldwater species, will eat almost anything of meat or vegetable origin, and they present relatively few problems as far as feeding is concerned.

Processed foods

Commercially available foods for fishes come in many different forms: flake, pellet, granular, powder, liquid, tablet, frozen and freeze-dried. Many of the flake forms are produced to different recipes, which take into consideration the varying needs of particular groups or species of fishes. Freeze-dried and frozen foods provide an occasional treat, and such foods as shellfish meat and small marine crustacea are eagerly taken by fishes in both pond and aquarium.

Adult feeding

Fry feeding

Left: *A selection of dried foods (clockwise from top left).*
1 *Multiflavoured flake.* **2** *Pellets.*
3 *Freeze-dried Tubifex.* **4** *Powdered.*
5 *Tablet.* **6** *Granular.* **7** *Freeze-dried shrimp.* **8** *Vegetable flake food.*

Above: *Foods in use:* 1 *Slow-sinking flakes.* 2 *Floating pellets.* 3 *Freeze-dried cube.* 4 *Stick-on-tablet.* 5 *Fast-sinking granular.* 6 *Powdered dry food.* 7 *Liquid fry food.*

The fishkeeper should bear in mind the feeding characteristics of his fishes so that food may be presented correctly for each species. Flake and pellet foods remain on the water surface for some time and are ideal for surface-feeding species. Granular and tablet foods may sink too fast for surface feeders but will be welcomed by bottom-dwelling fishes.

In an aquarium, the amount of food taken can be accurately assessed by watching the fishes at feeding time, and of course the whole depth of the aquarium can be monitored. In a pond, however, only those fishes feeding at the surface can be seen, and the fishkeeper has no idea how much food remains uneaten further down in the water. Overfeeding the fishes is a dangerous practice, as uneaten food will decay and begin to pollute the water. Uneaten food in an aquarium can be seen and removed, but in a pond it is a different matter. During the warm months of the year, the fishkeeper may wish to feed his fishes, to keep a link between himself and them, and also to be able to see them when he wishes; but such feeds should be small, so that the fishes hunt out the rest of the natural food in the pond for themselves. In this way the risk of pollution from overfeeding can be minimized.

A general rule is only to feed as much food as the fishes will take in five minutes. Food can be given perhaps three times a day for aquarium fishes throughout the year (remembering to ring the changes between different brands of food, to provide variety). Pond fishes can be fed small amounts during the day, but this should be adjusted according to season, water temperature and the presence or otherwise of suitable natural food in the pond.

Live foods

Aquarium fishes do not have access to the same amount of live foods that pond fishes do, and again must rely on the fishkeeper to provide this. Live foods include both waterborne and terrestrial animals, which can be collected and cultured by the fishkeeper.

Aquatic live foods include *Daphnia, Cyclops, Gammarus,* mosquito larvae, bloodworm larvae and even small tadpoles. Such food can be collected from ponds or rain butts during the appropriate season. If you collect live foods from the wild, take care to screen such foods thoroughly so that predatory insect larvae are not inadvertently introduced into the aquarium or pond.

Tubifex worms occur in polluted sewage-infested waters and should be thoroughly cleaned (by washing in continuous running water for a few days) before feeding them to the fishes. To prevent the worms burying themselves in the aquarium gravel or pond floor, feed them to the fishes by means of a floating worm feeder, which enables fishes to take the worms more slowly and conveniently at the water surface.

A waterborne crustacean that provides a very valuable food source for young fishes is *Artemia salina* (the brine shrimp). Its eggs may be stored dry over long periods, but when immersed in salt water the eggs can be hatched into tiny young shrimps that are ideal as the first living food for fish fry. They are also completely disease-free, which may not always be the case with live foods collected from the wild.

Earthworms from the garden (but not from lawns or compost heaps treated with insecticides or fertilizers) make excellent food, as also do members of the Enchytraeidae family. These small white worms, ranging from minute proportions to stout thread size, are ideal food for young fishes and may be cultured in soil-filled boxes and fed on cereal foods. A new culture is started from a portion of one about to end, and in this way a continuous supply can be maintained. One advantage of cultured foods (particularly those of

Above: *Tubifex worms, an ideal fish food, are usually collected from polluted waters (1) and must be cleaned by keeping them under running water for some time (2) before feeding them to fish. Use a floating worm feeder (3) for surface feeders and to prevent the worms from burrowing into the gravel.*

Below: *The larva of this Great Diving Beetle* (Dytiscus marginalis) *must be kept out of aquariums and ponds; it will attack small fishes.*

Right: *Hatching and feeding brine shrimp.*
1 *Empty a teaspoonful of brine shrimp eggs into a jar of salt water prepared by dissolving 30gm/litre (5oz/gallon) of natural salt, NOT table salt, in fresh water. (The amount of salt can be scaled down to suit the jar size if you do not want a litre of salt water, but you may need this much to maintain a continuous supply of shrimps).*

2 *Keep the solution at 24°C (75°F) and aerate strongly until hatching.*

3 *Collect hatched shrimps in fine net and rinse through with fresh, not salt, water.*

4 *Feed to fish. Salt water left from hatching jar can be re-used once or twice.*

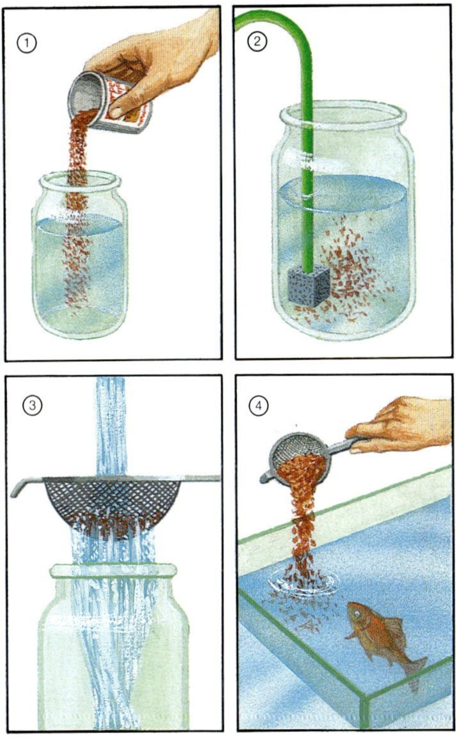

Below: *Dragonfly larvae will attack tiny fishes. Screen wild-caught live foods against predators before using them in ponds and aquariums.*

terrestrial origin) is that they can contain no disease that is communicable to the fishes. Wingless fruit-flies *(Drosophila)* and maggots can also be used to fill out the variety of live foods given.

Other sources of food

Canned pet food such as that given to cats and dogs is a useful addition to the fishes' menu, but do not use this type of food too heavily, in case you pollute the water. Lean meat (raw or cooked, excluding the grease and fatty parts) is also a good food, and liver and scraped ox-heart provide many a fish with its staple diet. Vegetable foods such as spinach, lettuce, green peas and wheatgerm will also be appreciated, and the inclusion of these vegetarian ingredients may well help to save some of the aquarium plants from being nibbled.

There is practically no limit to what food you can educate your fishes to accept, but never overfeed.

Maintenance

One of the unexpected pleasures of fishkeeping is the relatively small amount of time that needs to be spent on tiresome chores. It is true that a certain amount of regular servicing must be done, but even this can be very enjoyable, as once the chore is completed it is so easy to drop into a little 'fishgazing' immediately afterwards!

Regular checks
Top of the list of tasks will be the daily count of the fishes. This is an easy task with aquarium fishes (even possible from a nearby armchair), but a little more difficult with pond specimens; in summer they are hard to spot among the plants, and in winter they are well down in the warmer zone of the water, and only the most zealous fishkeeper will regularly venture far from the warmth of the house. The most convenient time to count the fish population is at feeding times, in whatever environment the fishes are being kept. If a previously good 'timekeeper' fails to make an appearance over a few days, then a search should be made for the absentee to see if anything is wrong. If a fish is sick or has died, it should be removed either for treatment or for disposal of the body. More positive signs can also be looked for, especially as the fishes start to breed and spawning is anticipated.

MAINTENANCE CHECK	Daily	Weekly	Monthly	Periodically
Check number of fishes	●	●	●	●
Water condition Check pH				●
Partial change of water			●	
Filters Box filter: Clean and replace medium according to amount of use and state of aquarium				●
Undergravel filter: Rake the aquarium gravel gently				●
Plants Remove dead leaves and excess sediment on leaves; thin out floating plants		●	●	●
Prune; replant cuttings and runners as necessary		●	●	●
General Check air supply carefully; clean air pump valves and air pump filter				●
Clean cover glass				●
Remove algae from front glass of aquarium				●
Check fishes for symptoms of diseases				●

Note: If your fishes start to behave oddly, it may be worth checking over the tasks outlined above – regular aquarium maintenance can keep them healthy.

Above: *Magnetic algae-scrapers remove algae easily from the glass and are quite covenient – they are always where you leave them!*

Above: *Siphoning off and replacing about 20% of the aquarium water every three weeks will help to maintain it in tip-top condition.*

Water level is also easy to check. In the aquarium it should not fall below the decorative trim, or the light from the hood will shine out through the gap and spoil the look of the aquarium. A falling water level can indicate excessive evaporation and a build-up of dissolved salts in the water. In lined ponds any unnecessary expanse of liner left exposed above the water will be liable to rot and crack under the influence of sunlight; this is particularly the case with polythene. The cascade or waterfall watercourse should be checked to see that it remains unobstructed and that the water keeps to its appointed route on the way back to the pond. (A falling water level in a pond does not always mean a leak through the liner.) It is also best to remove any fallen leaves that have got into the pond.

Plants also need to be inspected; remove any dead leaves and trim back excessive growth. Keep a keen eye on the pond or aquarium to see that no growths of algae are allowed to take hold; removing it at the first sign is far easier than leaving it until later, by which time it will be too late and you will have an unenviable task on your hands. A slender stick or branch can be used to twirl through the water to collect any filamentous algae like green candy-floss.

Cuttings may be taken from the plants, and planted elsewhere in the tank or used to set up another aquarium. Excessive growth of plants in the pond should usually be thinned out, although a dense growth of plants makes a good spawning medium in the breeding season.

The flow of water through the filter must remain at the normal rate. Any slowing indicates a clogged filter medium. The filter medium should be regularly renewed (although it is possible to re-use filter medium once or twice, after a thorough washing), and the gravel bed lightly raked over.

The main attention in the aquarium should be the regular partial water changes; approximately 20% of the water needs to be changed every three weeks or so. Replace it by water of the same temperature and quality, if possible. In summer months, the fishes may welcome more frequent changes of cooler water, as long as it is not too icy.

The front glass of the aquarium should be kept clean of algae, although a little growth on the remaining tank walls may be left for the fishes to browse on. Cover glasses must be kept spotlessly clean so as not to impede the light from reaching the aquarium plants. Raise the hood slightly in warm weather to dissipate heat from the lamps.

Plants in the pond may also be denied light in summer by excessive coverage of the water surface by the growth and unchecked spread of water lilies, and in winter by snow on the frozen pond. In either case, clear part of the water surface.

In severe winters, make a hole in the ice on the pond (by melting it, not by hammering) and keep it free to allow air to reach the water surface. Electric pond heaters are available to create an 'open circle' in the ice. The water level can be lowered to keep a layer of air below the ice, but this only works in a pond with sloping sides; in other cases, with vertical walls, the ice simply floats down with the water.

Coping with emergencies

Fortunately, there are few instances where the situation gets so bad that desperate action needs to be taken. It is a sign of bad management if the aquarium or pond requires complete dismantling because of unhealthy fishes, and such occurrences are the result of neglect by a lazy fishkeeper.

The remedy for very bad conditions is a rapid removal of the stock (both fishes and plants) to a new location while things are put right. Lower the water level in the pond so that the fishes may be caught more easily; don't forget to search the mud at the bottom of the pond for any bottom-dwelling fishes.

Also clean the pond filter. Any mechanical filtration can be cleaned with tapwater, but be sure to rinse biological filtration thoroughly with old pond water to preserve the aerobic bacteria. When refilling the pond, treat the tapwater with a conditioner and a bacterial starter product to aid the re-establishment of the filter. Apply these same principles when stripping down an aquarium to avoid water quality problems for the livestock. When restocking the pond or aquarium, float the fish in a bag as if introducing them for the first time, so that they can adjust to the different water chemistry and temperature. Carrying out regular maintenance should avoid the need to strip down either a pond or an aquarium.

Adding water lilies

Planting a water lily is easier than choosing the colour and size you want. Before choosing a water lily, take into account the size of the pond, the water depth and the amount of sun it receives. When buying a lily, look for rich green leaves (not brown slimy ones) with no yellowing at the edges. The crown should be hard, as this is where the plant stores its food during winter. Always buy lilies potted in aquatic baskets with the roots growing out through the sides; newly potted ones may take some time to settle down again. Small lilies should be planted in 3-4 litre pots, medium ones in 5-10 litre pots and large ones in 10 litre pots or larger.

Good aquatic centres will display the plants in shallow tanks at least 30cm (12in) deep. Avoid water lilies kept in plastic boxes but not in water. These can dry out and may even get mould on them, from which they rarely recover. If a particular plant looks healthy, then it probably is; if it looks poorly, do not buy it.

1 *When you first put the water lily in its basket on the bottom of your pond, the leaves may not be able to float on the surface. You can use a clean, upturned plastic pot to raise the lily up to the correct height. A black pot or bucket will be less visible in the water.*

Larger plants to create an instant display

Many aquatic centres sell larger, more mature specimens of water lilies – often with flowers – in 10 litre pots or larger. If you cannot wait a year or two for smaller ones to mature, these larger plants are a good buy that offer instant surface coverage and the bonus of flowers, too. The range of varieties available in larger sizes tends to be limited, so do not buy one if it is not the variety or size you really want. Planting an unsuitable one may cause problems and disappointment later on if it grows too large or does not fit into the colour scheme of the pond. If you are in any doubt, be patient and wait for a smaller one to mature.

2 *To wash surplus soil from the basket, make sure that the lily is thoroughly watered before you place it in the pond. Also add a generous layer of gravel to the surface to stop your fish digging out the soil and disturbing the plant as it becomes established in the pond.*

3 *With the lily in the pond, the leaves should be about 4cm (1.5in) below the water to allow them to grow to the surface. Depending on the temperature and variety, you will need to lower the lily every month so that eventually the basket is resting on the bottom.*

Fish anatomy

Until you start keeping fishes you may well think that one fish looks exactly like another, but very soon you will find out that there are many variations on the standard shape. Each variation has evolved over many years and generations of fishes, as Nature constantly refines the design, which is adapted to suit the fish's environment and feeding style.

A fish with a large body surface area is suitable for only slow-running or still waters; it could not cope with strong water currents. A fat cylindrical fish would not be at home among dense reed-beds, where a slim species would be. An upturned mouth is ideal for taking food from the water surface, but not from the river floor. Barbels (complete with taste-sensing cells) around the underslung mouth of a bottom-dwelling fish, coupled with large eyes, enable the animal to find its food in dark muddy waters and to be aware of any predators lurking close by.

Scales

Scales provide streamlining and protection for the body against injury. They grow constantly as the fish matures, and growth in a fish can be determined by noting the extra rings around each scale. However, these rings are not necessarily annual growth rings as with a tree, but are dependent on the seasons and the supply of food.

Fins

Fins are used for locomotion and stability, and, in some fishes, as spawning aids, either in courtship ritual displays or as egg-carriers, reproductive organs or water impellers over deposited eggs.

Generally, fishes have seven fins: three single and two pairs. The *anal* fin and *dorsal* fin act as stabilizers, and some species, such as the Perch *(Perca fluviatilis),* may have two dorsal fins. The tail or *caudal* fin provides the main forward thrust to drive the fish through the water. The paired *pelvic,* or *ventral,* and *pectoral* fins are used for manoeuvring, braking and adjusting the position of the fish in the water in much the same way as the hydroplanes on a submarine. They may also be used to perform fanning duties for removing dirt from eggs. The *pelvic* fins of some bottom-dwelling fishes are fused together to form a suction cup that prevents the fish from being swept away by water currents. In some tropical fishes there is an extra fin found between the dorsal and the caudal fin; this is the

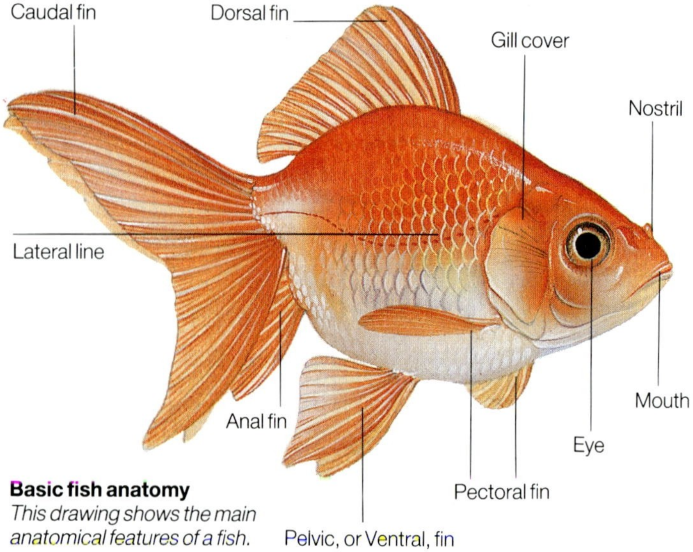

Basic fish anatomy
This drawing shows the main anatomical features of a fish.

adipose fin, a small fatty tissue structure, the purpose of which is not clear. Most fins are supported by hard rays, and in many instances the male can erect its dorsal fin at will to display to the female of the species or to threaten rival males.

Fishes cultivated in the aquarium and the pond often have exaggerated finnage, developed by intensively controlled selective breeding programmes; such finnage would not be found on fishes in the wild state, as the extra-long flowing fins would be more of a hindrance to the fish than an advantage.

Senses

The fish has the same five senses that we enjoy, although it differs in that its nostrils are used solely for smelling and not for breathing. Fishes can hear, but they also have the ability to sense very low frequency vibrations in the water by means of their *lateral line* system; this can be seen as a row of tiny holes in the scales along the sides of the fish, and vibrations are detected by the nervous system connected to these holes. Whisker-like growths called *barbels* are often found around the mouth in bottom-dwelling species and these help the fish to detect its food by taste rather than by sight.

Swim-bladder

Most fishes have a hydrostatic buoyancy organ that automatically adjusts itself to give the fish neutral density, and so allows it to remain at any chosen depth in the water.

Colour

Fishes use colour in many ways: it may attract a mate, assist in species recognition, or be a very useful means

Above: *This blue Japanese carp has little guanin below the skin but has retained a line of sparkling scales.*

of camouflage; it may even be used as a warning to other fishes to keep off; and it certainly attracts fishkeepers. Colour is produced in the fish in two ways: by reflection and by pigmentation.

Colour produced by reflection relies on *guanin,* a waste substance that is not excreted from the body but stored just beneath the skin, forming a light-reflecting layer. What colour light is reflected, ie what colour the fish presents to us, depends on how the crystals of guanin are aligned.

In Goldfishes, this layer of guanin may be present to give the familiar metallic look; or it may lie deeper in the skin, giving the impression that the fish has a mother-of-pearl sheen; or it may be lacking altogether, giving a matt finish.

Colour due to pigmentation can also lie at various depths in the skin; and the combinations of pigmentation hues with the three 'finishes' described above (to say nothing of the finnage development possibilities) give very ample scope for genetic experimentation in Goldfish breeding. Fishes can alter the apparent distribution of pigmentation, and at times the colours may be heightened or faded depending on their mood. As one would expect, the onset of breeding will be signalled by the intensifying of colour and the displaying of fins. An extra clue to the imminence of breeding is the development of small white pimples (tubercles) on the pectoral fins and gill plates of the male fishes, often mistaken as disease symptoms by some fishkeepers.

Diseases, cures and prevention

Despite the very best of intentions on the part of the fishkeeper, disease will strike eventually. To keep fishes in the best of health depends on everything being in tip-top condition at all times, and this means right from the very beginning. The main part of this Guide has dealt with how to set up and maintain the most favourable of environments for the fishes; the next logical step is to choose only the most healthy stock to inhabit the aquarium or pond. Even then, however, there is no guarantee that everything will be perfect, and so the fishkeeper must also learn how to recognize diseases, how to treat them and, just as important, how to prevent them breaking out again. Fortunately we all learn by our mistakes, but it is a pity that sometimes the fishes have to suffer while we are doing so.

Prevention

Select healthy stock and quarantine all new introductions until you are sure that they are free from any ailment. This is a rule that should be adhered to rigidly at all times, with no exceptions.

When choosing fishes, look for tell-tale signs of ill-health or anything that might spell trouble in the future. Fishes should be able to swim without undue effort and to remain at any position in the water. Fins should be erect and clear from ragged edges, spots, pimples or signs of fraying. There is a subtle difference between a fish that is swimming poorly due to sickness and one that is just simply overburdened by exaggerated finnage, but only experience will bring the ability to distinguish the one from the other. The colour of the fish should be dense, with the patterning well-defined; although patterning that is not well-defined may not be due to ill-health, such a fish would not be worth buying if a breeding programme was to be undertaken, as defects in the colour patterning would be passed on to the young. Fishes with deformed body shapes, hollow bellies, knife-edge backs, cloudy eyes, or open wounds are all best avoided. Do not buy any fish from a tank containing any dead or diseased fishes, no matter how smitten you are with that one that looks perfect.

If you are in any doubt about the requirements of your fishes as to water conditions, the dealer should be able to tell you about the water conditions in his tanks.

Transporting fishes can prove to be a traumatic experience for them, and they should be introduced into their new home with as little fuss and shock as possible.

Coldwater fishes need to be acclimatized to the temperature of their new aquarium; the transportation container can be either stood in the room or floated in the aquarium until the two water temperatures have equalized. (Remember, coldwater fishes' aquarium water temperature varies with the ambient air temperature, and is not constant as in the tropical aquarium.) Pond fishes can be floated in a bucket or plastic bowl before they are released into the pond.

The above presumes that the fishes brought home are your first purchases and will, in fact, be quarantined in their new home. When adding new fishes to the collection, set up a spare tank in which a new fish can be kept for two or three weeks before being put in with your other fishes. During this time, any latent disease should manifest itself and can be treated, thus avoiding any possibility of passing on infection.

Treatment of diseases

Fish diseases are fairly easy to recognize and usually the victim

Above left: *This Goldfish has severe lesions on the head.* Above right: *The scale damage evident here probably results from poor handling.*

responds to treatment very well. Many of the aquatic food and equipment manufacturers also produce remedies for fish diseases and these are extremely well-packaged with easy-to-follow directions.

The process by which a sick fish can be restored to full health again should follow these lines: recognition that the fish is sick; removal of the fish to a hospital tank; further observation of the symptoms to determine the cause of the sickness; treatment; acclimatization of the fish back to the normal aquarium or pond water conditions; returning the fish to the collection.

Once again, it is the result of constant observation of the fishes by the fishkeeper that builds up a knowledge of what is normal and what is not. Any fish exhibiting unusual behaviour such as gasping at the water surface, developing an excessive covering of skin mucus,

Below: *This fish is not in the best of health. Note the spot on the anal fin and signs of the top lobe of the caudal fin being eaten away.*

repeatedly scratching against rocks or plants, showing fading colours or a swollen profile, or not feeding or swimming as expected, should be removed for observation.

The hospital tank should be equipped with a filter system (no activated carbon, which will adsorb any medication used) and an aeration system (some medications may lower the oxygen content of the water). Depending on the ailment, the fish can be treated externally (for wounds and parasites) or the whole tank can be treated. The treatment required is indicated under each individual entry in the section that follows. The concentration of stock solutions may vary from country to country, and if you are in any doubt about the strength of the medication seek advice from a qualified chemist or veterinarian.

Some common diseases

Anchor worm

This is an external parasite *(Lernaea)* that can be seen with the naked eye. Remove it with tweezers or kill it with a solution of potassium permanganate or modern anti-parasite treatment. If a wound is left on the fish, bath it with iodine. Remove anchor worms as soon as they are seen, otherwise a colony will build up in the pond or aquarium, which will be difficult to remove. Anchor worm is introduced to the pond or aquarium with new plants or live foods.

Dropsy

This is a difficult disease to cure but easy to diagnose. The fish's body becomes very swollen due to liquid accumulating in the body cavities; the cause is not yet agreed upon. Some fishes appear to cure themselves after a period of isolation. Some brave fishkeepers try to draw off the liquid with a syringe. Dropsy can be contagious, and if the fish does not recover in isolation it should be destroyed.

Eye infections

A cloudy eye may be due to a mass of tiny larval worms or to a bacterial infection. A cataract normally affects only one eye. Another form of eye

Slimy skin
Fishes afflicted with this condition develop a thin grey film over the body. The parasites *Cyclochaeta* and *Costia* (shown at below left, right) cause the fish to produce excessive amounts of slime.

Dropsy
The scales protrude noticeably due to accumulated liquid in the body. The fluid from infected fish may infect others. To prevent this happening remove any sick fishes promptly.

Fish diseases
This fish is unlucky to have all these ailments at once! Use this illustration as a diagnostic aid to help you recognize common disease symptoms and to prevent your fishes from ever reaching this sorry state.

Tailrot/Finrot
These very obvious symptoms appear on fishes of poor health. Physical damage and unhygienic conditions in the aquarium or pond all encourage the harmful bacterial action.

White spot
Tiny white spots cover the fins and body. A common parasitic ailment that some aquarists believe lies dormant in every aquarium or pond ready to afflict weak fishes.

Skin flukes
The *Gyrodactylus* parasites burrow into the fish's skin and stay near the surface. Affected fishes lose colour and become feeble. Responds well to treatments.

Eye infections
Cloudy eyes (below) are often due to larval worms, cataract or bacterial infection. Protruding eyes (main drawing) usually suggests that other diseases are present as well.

Fungus
Fungus *(Saprolegnia)* attacks fishes already weakend by physical damage, parasites, or poor conditions. Also liable to affect fishes if they are transferred to widely differing pond or aquarium waters.

Gill flukes
The flatworm *(Dactylogyrus)* attaches itself to the gill membranes. Affected fishes have faster respiration and gaping gills.

Mouth 'fungus'
This is caused by a bacterial infection. It is important to catch this infection as soon as it appears. Use an anti-bacterial treatment.

disease is known as exophthalmia, where the eye protrudes greatly from its socket. Treatment for such diseases is very much 'hit and miss'. Proprietary remedies for cloudy eyes, iodine and glycerine treatment for cataracts and clean water conditions for exophthalmia have all been successful to some degree.

Finrot
This affliction starts upon physically damaged fins after bad handling techniques (by the fishkeeper) or bullying (by other fishes). It is encouraged in poor water conditions. The tissue between the fin rays can be seen to be rotting away. Proprietary remedies will help to cure the symptoms but not the causes, which remain the responsibility of the fishkeeper.

Fish louse
A parasite appearing as spots up to 8mm (0.3in) across on the body and fins, the fish louse (*Argulus*) should be treated as for anchor worm.

Flukes
Flukes may attack the skin of fishes *(Gyrodactylus)* or the gill membranes *(Dactylogyrus)*. Skin flukes cause the fishes constantly to scratch themselves against rocks, plant pots or even the gravel floor. Gill flukes cause inflamed gill membranes and a rapid increase in respiration rates. Both parasites (up to 0.8mm/0.03in long) may be treated with well-aerated solutions of proprietary treatments specially formulated for parasitic control, such as Paratox.

Fungus
This is seen either as an outbreak of cotton-wool tufts over the body, or as an overall covering of a cobweb-like substance. Proprietary remedies are now convenient to use and very effective against this condition.

Gasping
This is not a disease, but an indication that something is wrong in the water conditions, probably low oxygen levels. It is quite often seen in thundery weather with pond fishes, and steps should be taken to increase the aeration and water turbulence at the water surface to drive out the carbon dioxide. Increasing the number of oxygenating plants will only make things worse, because they will increase the amount of carbon dioxide in the water during the hours of darkness. After things have returned to normal keep the water conditions in better shape, and an eye on the weather.

Mouth fungus
This is caused not by the same agent

Below: *The fish louse* (Argulus) *– up to 8mm (0.3in) long – has buried deep into the skin of this Goldfish and will be difficult to remove.*

as fungus *(Saprolegnia)* but by a bacterial infection. Be sure to tackle this promptly using a modern anti-bacterial treatment.

Shimmying

The name is very descriptive of the movements made by the fish when afflicted. The condition is brought about by stress or by chilling. A period of gradually increasing water temperature in a separate aquarium will alleviate the condition until the fish returns to normal health.

White spot

This is the most common fish disease, easily recognized and easily treated with proprietary remedies. The fish is covered with tiny white spots; but do not confuse these spots with the white turbercles seen on the gill covers of male Goldfishes in the breeding season. The disease (caused by the parasite *Ichthyophthirius*) is best treated when it is off the fish, in the free-swimming stage of its life cycle. As most fishes in the collection will succumb, the whole aquarium should be treated. Remember to increase the aeration. In some instances, certain delicate-leaved plants may be adversely affected by the remedy.

Below: *This parasitic anchor worm* (Lernaea) *is slightly more visible than the fish louse (up to 2cm/0.8in long) and can be treated similarly.*

Internal diseases

Internal diseases are much harder to diagnose, since by the time the symptoms are visible it may be too late to save the fish. For the curious, an after-death investigation might reveal the diseases, and there are several mail order diagnostic services available. The new inexperienced fishkeeper may wish to live in ignorance of this aspect of the hobby for the time being!

Above: *The infection cycle for white spot disease.* **1** *The afflicted fish shows the symptoms and the parasites leave the body.* **2** *Cysts form on the tank floor.* **3** *The cysts produce free-swimming parasites.*

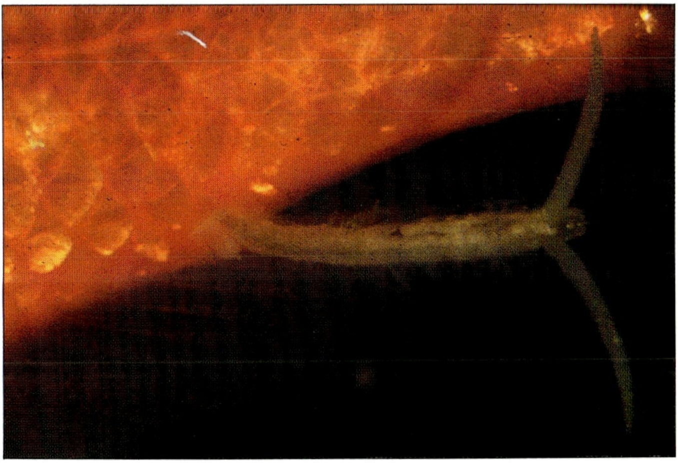

Breeding

The breeding of fishes in captivity may be seen as the pinnacle of the hobby, the fishes' final accolade to the owner that everything is just right, and it is here that you cease being just a fishkeeper and perhaps deserve the lofty title of aquarist.

Reasons for breeding ornamental fishes are many. Some people earnestly believe that they can make a living from it; but enthusiastic amateurs, though realizing that they can't, will nevertheless spend years striving to produce their own version of the perfect fish. To some fishkeepers, it may just happen in the anonymity of the pond in the garden; and to others it may never happen at all. Here are some helpful hints.

Successful spawning

To have a successful spawning of fishes, you must start with a true pair, and they must be in the right frame of mind and condition. The spawning conditions must also be correct, and the aquarium is the best place so that you can keep things under control, see what's going on and check results. It may be a little more difficult to provide the ideal conditions necessary for spawning to occur in an aquarium, as opposed to the more natural environment of the pond, but it can be done with care and feeding.

In nature and in the pond the onset of spring followed by the warmer summer provides the stimulus for spawning. At the same time, the

Left: *A male Stickleback energetically fans the eggs that have been laid in a tunnel nest built from plant fragments. He guards them until they hatch.*

Above: *The tubercles on the gill plates and pectoral fins of this Goldfish show that it is in a breeding condition, not diseased as might be supposed.*

amount of live natural foods also increases, and this brings the adult fishes into the peak of condition. After spawning occurs, there is still plenty of time for the fry to grow and feed before the cold months come around again, and they can build up their reserves to overwinter successfully.

In the aquarium, it is possible to simulate the conditions of nature to a certain extent, by artificially heating the water a few degrees as your planned spawning time approaches. By this time, the pair will have been selected and brought to peak condition. One advantage of aquarium breeding is that you can choose which fishes to breed with, whereas in a pond the fishes will spawn as the mood takes them.

Fishes for breeding should be chosen for their colour, fins and body shape; these qualities may be spread between the two fishes if neither has all the desirable features. The best (and the worst) will be passed on to the young. This is true for any species of fish, but in this section we shall be concentrating more on the breeding of the Goldfish; breeding notes for other species will be found in the second half of this Guide.

Sexing Goldfishes is not too difficult. The male fish develops tubercles on the gill covers and the first rays of the pectoral fins as breeding time approaches. The female fish fills with eggs and takes on a more rounded appearance. Observation of the vents of the fishes will show that the female's is larger and may even protrude a little.

Before spawning is planned to occur, separate the sexes and feed the fishes a wide variety of predominantly live foods. In limited spaces the two fishes can share a divided tank, and often this helps to ensure that the reunion is all the more successful.

The spawning tank should be fairly roomy, 100 litres (22 gallons) or so, and furnished with clumps of bushy egg-catching plants or artificial spawning mops made of nylon wool strands tied in a bundle. The male will drive the female into these clumps, and eggs will be trapped in them and hidden from the adult fishes, who would otherwise probably eat them. The adult fishes can be removed after spawning and the eggs left in the mops to hatch; or the mops can be removed to another convenient tank and the eggs hatched there. Eggs hatch in about four days at a temperature of 21°C (70°F), but take longer at lower temperatures.

Above: *A pair of fishes can be conditioned before spawning quite easily in a single tank by using a simple glass partition as here.*

Care of the fry

When the fry hatch, they will not need food immediately, as they take a little while to absorb the yolk sac; but they will need food as soon as they have become free-swimming. Any addition of food to the water before this time is both unnecessary and dangerous, as the uneaten food will contaminate the tank. First foods can be cultivated infusoria cultures (microscopic single-celled animals, such as *Paramecium*) or one of the proprietary brands of liquid or powdered fry foods; but infusoria-culturing can be a smelly business (with no guarantee of success, either), so it pays to have a proprietary food available anyway.

The idea is to have the young fry almost literally swimming in food and feeding around the clock. To this end, the fry-raising aquarium can be dimly lit at all times to encourage fry activity,

Below: *Dense clumps of plants, or a tangle of nylon wool, make excellent egg-traps in the aquarium for egg-scattering fishes such as Goldfish.*

which naturally will include feeding. A close watch must be kept on water conditions; supply light aeration and use a simple sponge filter, and make careful partial water changes.

As the fry grow they can take food of larger particle size and at this time there is no better food than the brine shrimp *(Artemia salina)*, the culture of which is described on page 49. From here on, it is a matter of keeping the fry well fed and well spread out if there is a very large number of them. They can be culled from time to time; discard the deformed or tiny ones, or those that do not conform to the accepted standard.

Breeding of the quality Goldfish in its many varieties is a time-consuming business and needs to be a well-coordinated procedure. Do not try to breed a few of each variety, but narrow your interest down to one or two varieties and concentrate on

Above: *In this collection of young Goldfishes, the two fishes at the surface have yet to change into the familiar gold colours shown by their companions. Generally, Goldfish turn gold after about one year, but some never do. This does not necessarily mean that they are diseased.*

breeding them as well as you can. Keep the strain pure, do not allow poor quality fishes to degrade your efforts, and always keep a record of what you do, so that any successes can be repeated without having to go back to square one again.

Sophisticated line-breeding procedure, along with hand-stripping of the fish for breeding (stroking the female fish so that she releases her eggs), are outside the sphere of this Guide and the reader is directed to the more specialist literature for information on these subjects.

Goldfishes

The Goldfish has a 'pedigree' of something approaching 1,000 years as a cultivated animal, although we cannot be any more accurate than that. Authorities who have researched the history of the species all agree that it was somewhere around AD 1000 during the Sung era in China, that this fish began to gain popularity, although there is an even earlier mention of the fish in poetry from about AD 800.

From this origin, the Goldfish was first taken eastwards to Japan, where it continued to grow in popularity, although this first excursion was to take 500 years. By the end of the seventeenth century, the species had become widespread throughout the East as an ornamental fish.

Westerners had to wait a little longer for the Goldfish; although the diarist Samuel Pepys remarks on 'coloured fishes' being kept in 1665, there is no evidence to identify them accurately, and they may well have been a hardy tropical species such as the Paradisefish (*Macropodus opercularis*). Other sources give the years 1611, 1691 and 1728 as the time when the Goldfish reached Europe. By now, interest in scientific things was growing rapidly and many papers were written which included the Goldfish; among these was von Linné's *Systema Naturae* in which the

Above: *The common ancestry between the Common Goldfish* (Carassius auratus) *and this Crucian Carp can be seen quite clearly.*

Goldfish was first classified as *Cyprinus auratus*. Goldfishes reached the Netherlands from Italy, and specimens imported from England were soon being bred in the Netherlands too. Perhaps the first fish exhibition was in Russia in 1791, when the Winter Gardens were decorated with Goldfishes in bowls during a banquet given by Prince Gregory Alexandrovitch for Catherine the Great. Finally, the Goldfish reached America, around the end of the nineteenth century.

Taxonomics of the Goldfish

The Goldfish belongs to the Cyprinidae (the Carp family), and is one of the two species in the genus *Carassius* (the other species is *C. carassius*, the Crucian Carp). For many years it was believed that the Goldfish (*C. auratus*) was descended from the Crucian Carp as a colour variant, but now it is generally accepted that the two species are quite separate. There is also a sub-species, *C. auratus gibelio* (the European Prussian Carp), and it has a mixture of Crucian and Goldfish characteristics.

Colour in Goldfish

Much of the attraction of Fancy Goldfishes lies in the wide variety of their colours. We have seen earlier that these colours are due to the amount of reflection given by the layer of guanin beneath the skin (see Anatomy page 54). Three groups of scale effect have been internationally recognized: *Metallic* (maximum reflectivity), *Nacreous* (scales visible but with a pearly sheen) and *Matt* (scales appear to be non-existent, and the fish looks dull). These scale properties may be present in any variety, but rigid standards set up by serious-minded hobbyists and commercial breeders have restricted certain reflectivities to certain forms of fish to protect the purity of the strains so painstakingly developed.

Types of Goldfish

Because of its longevity, hardiness and willingness to breed, the Goldfish is the perfect inhabitant for aquarium or pond, and over the years since its introduction, many different varieties have been developed. Left to its own devices, however, the Goldfish would soon revert back to a very dull-coloured fish reminiscent of its near relative; the creation of these many varieties is due entirely to the work and ambitions of fishkeepers.

Tropical fishkeepers are almost obsessed with the size that their fishes attain (because they gain points according to size at exhibitions and shows), but the Goldfish fancier is not so influenced by this criterion because the size of the fish is not taken into consideration during judging. This is because the Goldfish's size is very dependent upon its environment, aquarium or pond, and the size can therefore vary greatly as a result.

Goldfish varieties can be divided into two convenient groups, Singletails and Twintails; each group has sub-divisions according to colour, fin form and body shape. The following varieties of Goldfish are all internationally recognized.

Right: *A group of healthy Goldfishes. Note their slightly down-turned mouths, indicating bottom-feeding.*

Singletails

In general, the body proportions of singletailed Goldfishes are such that the body depth is always less than half the body length, with the head proportion (usually less than one third of the body length) being excluded from this equation.

Common Goldfish

If being the pride and joy, and family pet, through many generations the world over entitles the fish to the back-handed compliment of being called 'common', then so be it; but surely the fish that put most of us on the road to aquarium happiness deserves a better adjective?

This fish should have a thickset sturdy look, with the dorsal curve echoed by a similar curve to the ventral surface. The colour should be a dense red, red-orange, orange or yellow. Often a certain amount of silver is present, and many fishkeepers are very happy with this combination. The scales are highly metallic and cover the whole body from the rear of the head to the caudal fin. A truly handsome fish.

London Shubunkin

In over-simplified terms, the London Shubunkin is the Common Goldfish without the metallic scales; the scales are either nacreous or matt. The type with a blue body, with patches of red, yellow, violet, brown and black with black speckles, is very popular.

Bristol Shubunkin

The immediate visible difference between this variety and the last is

Below: *A Bristol Shubunkin showing many desirable features of its strain; blue, black, red and orange colours, and a finely spread caudal.*

Above: *The Common Goldfish. The dorsal curve is matched exactly by the ventral curve beneath. A very robust fish with excellent colour.*

Twintails

Fishes in this group have the caudal and anal fins paired or divided with each part equally developed. The body is more egg-shaped, with its depth more than half its length.

Within this group are the more exotic-finned, and to some deformed, body shapes created by the intensive breeding programmes of dedicated fishkeepers over many years. These varieties are not hardy enough to stand overwintering in a pond and should be brought indoors during the cold months of the year. They are probably more suitable for the aquarium anyway, where their extraordinary beauty can be seen more easily, and where they will be more secure and less at risk to cats, herons or any other form of life that might covet them as potential food.

Fantail

As its name suggests, the attraction of this fish is its tail; the top edge of the broad, shallow-forked caudal fin should not droop below the horizontal. Dorsal fin height when erect should be about half the body depth. There are both metallic and nacreous types of this fish.

Right: *The beauty of these Fantails is further enhanced by artistic planting.*

Below: *Fantails have egg-shaped bodies with divided caudal and anal fins. A spectacular looking fish.*

Above: *The Jikin's caudal fin is held stiffly and at right-angles to the body.*

Below: *A Pearlscale, with raised scales and symmetrical fins.*

Jikin

The Butterfly Tail, to give the fish its common name, is a shallow-bodied fish with only a moderate development of the caudal fin, the two halves of which are held erect and at right angles to the caudal peduncle. The ideal coloration is a silver metallic body with red lips and fins, but difficult to achieve.

Pearlscale

Many of the foregoing remarks for the Fantail apply to this variety, but the main feature is the appearance of the scales, which are domed; where the metallic body colour is red, the centre of the scales is lighter in colour and they appear to be 'pearly', hence the common name. Provide clean water for all Goldfish with flowing fins.

Above: *The Tosakin has an elegant caudal curving forward and upwards.*

Below: *When seen from above, the Tosakin's tail is equally impressive.*

Tosakin

The Peacock Tail is a most graceful metallic fish, with its caudal fin joined along the upper edge to produce a most complex curved effect. Many authorities handstrip this fish to spawn it (see Breeding page 65), as it appears to have difficulty doing it on its own, because its physical form restricts its swimming ability.

Veiltail

A high dorsal fin and a drooping, non-forked caudal fin are the identifying features of this fish. The flowing fins are prone to damage and infection, so this fish is best suited to the aquarium, where it can benefit from the best of clean and peaceful conditions. It can be metallic or nacreous. *(Illustrated overleaf)*

Moor

This is one of those fishes whose common name nearly everyone gets wrong! Because of its colour, the fish is often called the Black Moor, but in Goldfish circles the Moor is never any other colour but black. The deep black colour must spread right to the very edges of the fins. The fish is similar in shape and finnage to the Veiltail, but the eyes of this variety protrude from its head.

Left: *This young Moor, velvety black, has fine protruding eyes.*

Oranda

With this variety, emphasis is changed from the development of fins or protruding eyes to the head of the fish, where a raspberry-like growth appears as a hood. The fins have pointed ends. Good-quality fishes are usually seen in metallic configuration with a deep red-orange coloration. A striking appearance.

Below: *Even those who find genetic experimentation unnatural will appreciate the graceful and delicate beauty of this superb Oranda.*

Above: *Tancho Oranda. This variety has a red cap, but some fish are seen with only a pale yellow-orange cap.*

Inset above: *The Ranchu has a down-turned caudal peduncle. Note the extended 'hood' over the head and the absence of dorsal fin.*

Tancho Oranda

Just as the Tancho Singletail had a red cap added to the basic Comet features, so the Tancho Oranda is a colour variation of the Oranda; the body colour is metallic silver, but the red-orange cap is confined to the top of the head only.

Ranchu

The next development in breeding produced a Goldfish with no dorsal fin. The Ranchu is similar to the Lionhead but distinguished from it by the severely down-turned caudal pendunclе. The caudal fin shows to full effect when seen from above.

Lionhead *(Shown overleaf)*

The existing fins are short and stiffly held, and the hood is even more pronounced. In Japan there are several regional variations on this fish, all vigorously supported. The caudal fin of the Lionhead is best viewed from the rear of the fish.

Pompon

The common name refers to the development of the nostrils to give two 'pompons', which to the purist must be of equal development. In most other respects this metallic or nacreous fish resembles the Lionhead in body form and finnage, but the two 'pompons' have replaced the hood as this fish's main attraction.

Celestial

If you spend a lot of time looking at fishes, here is one that appears to be getting its own back. It has no dorsal fin and almost rudimentary remaining fins but just look at its eyes! Needless to say, this Goldfish variety is a little handicapped in the race for food, and how it captures live food below its horizon is something to wonder at. Obviously, this metallic or nacreous fish is best suited for aquarium life.

Bubble-eye

A further development from the Celestial, this variety has extra-extended sacs beneath its upward-gazing eyes, which wobble about when the fish is in motion. Because of the danger of damage to its delicate eye-sacs, this metallic variety is best kept in an aquarium.

Below: *Over-developed nostrils of the Pompon are a desirable feature.*

Bottom: *The Celestial, in which the fins take second place to those extraordinary upward-gazing eyes.*

Above and below: *These two pictures show the remarkable development of the Bubble-eye's main features. The bubble sacs are very delicate.*

Koi

Koi is the Japanese word for Carp, and Nishiki Koi, a name familiar to many Westerners, means Brocaded Carp. The word Goi is often used in fish literature, normally with a qualifying word preceding it, such as Ma Goi, the Wild Carp.

The Koi is a colour variant of the Carp (*Cyprinus carpio*) and, although related to the Goldfish by also being a member of the Cyprinidae family, it differs from the Goldfish both in overall size and by having two barbels at the corner of its mouth.

Again like the Goldfish, the Koi has its origins hidden in the mists of time, but it is likely that this fish was first kept as a food fish, and that any highly coloured specimens were subsequently singled out, first as pets and later as breeding stock for future generations of coloured fishes.

In Japan, space is often at a premium, and any pond may extend beneath the house. Little wonder that, being fed household scraps through a trapdoor in the living room floor, the fishes soon become tame and can be hand fed.

Another difference, from the fishkeeper's point of view (literally), is that these fish have been developed to present their best colour pattern when seen from above, swimming over the dark floor of the pond. Consequently, although young Koi may be kept in an indoor aquarium, it is not until they are released into an outdoor pond that their beauty can be seen to best advantage.

Today, Koi are appreciated and kept in all parts of the world and enormous sums of money change hands for a truly high-quality specimen. Specialist societies cater for those fishkeepers who wish to devote their total efforts to keeping this species, and these societies often organize trips to Japan to see the fish of their dreams in its original surroundings, the graceful tranquil gardens of the Orient.

Above: *Close up on a striking Koi.*

Right: *A Mirror Carp, with large shiny scales. Reaching Japan from Germany, it was called 'Doitsu', a name used for Koi with similar scales.*

Keeping Koi

Pond-kept specimens attain better colours and are more active than aquarium-kept fishes. Koi are foraging fishes and will soon muddy up a pond that has a gravel floor. They will also eat some of the plants, especially those with submerged leaves, but water lilies and floating plants with leaves on or above the surface are generally ignored. Although the fish will not mind cloudy

water conditions, the fishkeeper may feel that the pond looks better with a filtration system fitted.

Because they can grow quite large, a relatively big pond is necessary, and it should also be deep enough to enable the fishes to overwinter successfully. A water depth of 1.5m (5ft) is the absolute minimum for Koi. It is difficult to give any hard and fast rules about the number of fishes any pond will support, especially as most people will not buy fully grown Koi at the outset. Koi are not particularly territorial and will be quite happy in a crowd. Watch for the usual sign of overcrowding – fishes gasping at the surface, especially in warm or thundery weather – and if in any doubt, always understock the pond.

Varieties of Koi

As this is a single species, the only variation between fishes can be that of colour and colour patterning. There are many diverse combinations, each with its own apparently indecipherable Japanese name. However, just as with scientific names, these are founded on

commonsense rules, and are a nuisance only to those unwilling to learn. The Japanese names should be pronounced evenly, with every syllable sounded.

As with the fancy varieties of Goldfishes, there are internationally recognized colour patterns for Koi. Each colour on the fish should be dense and clearly defined from any surrounding colour. A selection of Koi is shown in the following pages together with a reference list of some of the more popular names and colour patterns available.

KOI CHARACTERISTICS

Colours

Aka	Red
Ao	Turquoise
Beni	Orange
Gin	Silver metallic
Hariwake	Gold and silver
Hi	Red
Hisoku	Yellow-green
Ki	Yellow
Kin	Gold metallic
Kohaku	Red and white
Kuro	Black
Muji	Self-coloured
Ohgon	Golden yellow
Sarasa	Multicoloured
Shiro	White
Shoku	Coloured
Sumi	Black

Patterns

Asagi	Light blue reticulated
Bekko	Tortoiseshell
Matsuba	Pine cone (scales)
Moyo	Patterned

Descriptive terms

Akame	Eye with red iris
Doitsu	Mirror-scaled
Goke	Scale
Kabuto	Cap, helmet
Karasu	Black as a crow
Kawa	Leather, hide
Kuchibeni	Red-lipped
Kujaku	Multicoloured (Peacock)
Meija	Era 1868-1912
Rin	Scale
Sanke, or Sanshoku	Three-coloured, usually red, black and white
Showa	Era from 1926-
Shusui	Old variety from 1868-1926
Sui	Water (rippling effect)
Taisho	Era 1912-1926
Tancho	A bird (Tancho zuru) with a red crest
Utsuri	Reflecting
Yamabuki	Japonica bush with pale yellow flowers. (Pale yellow colour.)

Below: *Shiro Bekko – a white fish with lovely tortoiseshell markings.*

Below: *Gin Rin Kohaku – a metallic scaled red and white fish.*

Above: *Matsuba Ohgon – golden yellow with pine cone scales.*

Left: *The varied colours of this group of Koi are more easily appreciated against a dark background.*

Below: *Koi in a pond, where their size and colours complement the above-the-water beauty of the water lily.*

Above: *Koi contrasts. Asagi – light blue reticulated with red fins and head; Kohaku – red and white.*

Below: *Koi in an exhibition aquarium provide an opportunity for everyone to see the fish from another angle.*

By selective breeding, colours and scale formations can be interchanged to give the wide combination of beautiful fish shown here.

Above left: *Ohgon – golden yellow.*

Above right: *Tancho Kohaku – a stunning red-capped white fish.*

Left: *Kin Ki Utsuri – a striking Koi of a golden reflecting metallic-yellow colouration. A superb fish.*

Below left: *Shusui – combining the features of an Asagi with a Doitsu.*

Below right: *Hariwake Ohgon – silver and golden yellow areas on the fish.*

Other suitable species

At the beginning of this Guide, the point was made that, to many people, coldwater fishkeeping meant Goldfishes or (by a further stretch of the imagination) Koi.

Over the past few years, many more fishkeepers have not only learnt of the existence of other fishes that can be kept successfully in aquariums or ponds, but have taken the trouble to seek out these species and gain practical experience for themselves. In doing so, they have made others more aware too, through showing these species at exhibitions, for instance. Here we present a few alternatives. In addition to the Goldfish and Koi, the following Cyprinid fishes

Below: *Golden Orfe are constantly active fish, always visible in the pond, often splashing at the surface. Keep them in a shoal of at least five.*

can be kept in an aquarium or pond. Although several species of native fishes can also be kept, most Water Authorities have a minimum size below which a fish may not be taken from a lake or river; it follows that even if you could take a large enough fish, it would be too large to keep in an aquarium, or would require very special conditions.

As a general rule, always understock rather than overstock the pond. This allows fish to breed up to the natural level, it reduces the risk of disease outbreaks and improves the growth rates of the fish.

Idus idus

The Golden Orfe is an active shoaling fish that delights in disporting itself in the upper waters of the pond. In an aquarium, this popular ornamental fish needs plenty of swimming space and a tightly fitting hood.

Rutilus rutilus

Like the Rudd, the Roach is an example of a coarse fish that has found its way into the ornamental pond. It is not quite as nervous as the Rudd, but in common with that fish, it can breed at an alarming rate if not checked. In spring, the head of the male is covered in white spots, known as a breeding rash. This is the best time to buy the fish as you can select all males or all females to

prevent them breeding. Roach are better suited to a wildlife pond, as they are not particularly colourful. Their average length is 20cm (8in) but they can grow to twice that size. They accept floating and live foods.

Above: *The Roach and the Rudd are often confused, but you can tell them apart by the position of the pelvic fins. In the Roach, the fins start in line with dorsal fin, but in Rudd they start before the dorsal fin.*

Scardinius erythrophthalmus

The Golden Rudd is a truly active but nervous fish that can unsettle other, calmer fish, such as Koi. Given plenty of swimming space, it is very successful in ponds and quickly multiplies. It is best confined to a sizable pond that can cope with a large number of fish. The fry are quite large when they are born and stand a good chance of survival. To

keep the numbers under control, remove excess fish when necessary. It is most often seen in the golden form; as in the Orfe, the natural fish is darker. Orfe and Rudd are often mistaken for each other.

Below: *Golden Rudd will eat any dried foods, but they prefer live foods, such as midge larvae and worms. Although surface feeders by nature, Golden Rudd can adapt to midwater and even bottom feeding.*

Tinca tinca

The so-called 'Doctor Fish', the Tench is a peaceful, often nocturnal bottom-dwelling species. At one time it was thought that its body mucus was in some way medicinally beneficial to other fishes, but there is no scientific support for this. Reproduction is accomplished in shoals in the wild, and the eggs are deposited on plants. This is a rather drab fish, and not always clearly seen, being a bottom-dweller; a gold variety exists, which may be a more alluring proposition to the fishkeeper.

Right: *Young specimens of the Tench may be kept in the aquarium, where they are more easily seen than in the depths of a pond.*

Below: *The Golden Tench is one of the best-looking fish for a small pond. It eats any dry food, but also appreciates sinking and live food, such as worms or maggots, plus sweet corn and wholemeal bread.*

Low-temperature-tolerant tropical species

A number of tropical species have a wide tolerance to temperature changes, and may be kept in home aquariums or small ponds during the summer months. The following species are good ones to try, and you may be surprised to find that their numbers have increased after their period in the sun: *Jordanella floridae, Macropodus opercularis, Oryzias javanicus, O. latipes* and *Tanichthys albonubes* (White Cloud Mountain Minnow). Some species of *Poecilia, Gambusia* or even *Xiphophorus*, the live-bearing fishes, may be tried.

Right: *The male White Cloud Mountain Minnow is slimmer and more colourful than the female. Under aquarium lights, the stripe down the flanks looks iridescent.*

Below: *Keep the elegant long-finned form of the White Cloud Mountain Minnow away from fin-nipping fish.*

Right: *The male dwarf topminnow* (Heterandria formosa) *rivals some marine gobies for the title of the 'world's smallest fish' (pictured here on the left). By bringing live young and not eggs into the world, female livebearers (pictured on the right), have increased the odds of survival many times over. Do not mix them with other fishes, however 'non-predatory' these may seem. A densely planted aquarium will suit them better, allowing them to reproduce undisturbed.*

Below left: *Female Mosquitofish* (Gambusia affinis) *are larger than males, and easy to tell apart by their unmodified anal fin and plumper body profile. The common name is well-deserved, as it has been introduced all over the world to control malarial mosquitoes.*

Below right: *The Medaka* (Oryzias latipes) *matches perfectly the yellow mud of its native rivers, against which a darker fish would stand out and be vulnerable to predators. Because of their small size, keep medakas either in a species aquarium or in the company of other fishes that will not want to eat them! Provide a well-planted tank with gentle, but efficient, filtration that fully circulates the water.*

Adding the fish

When you are ready to buy your first fish, go on a day when the weather is cool and, if possible, when the aquatic centre is not too busy so that you can see the fish and talk to a member of staff. Explain that they are for a new pond and buy just a few hardy Goldfish. Do not fill the pond with fish – give it time to settle down. The filter system must mature before it can deal with more than just a few fish.

Only buy fish that look healthy. Do not choose any individuals lying on their sides or any that stay away from the rest of the fish in a tank. In fact, avoid buying any fish in such a tank on the basis that if one is ill there is a strong possibility that the others are, too. Look for fish with a good colour and that are well fed; do not buy skinny fish. Look at the fish in the bag before you take them home. Are all the fins in good condition? Are there any marks on the fish? If you are doubtful about a particular fish, ask to change it. If you start with healthy fish, you will hopefully be able to keep and enjoy them for several years.

Below: *The dealer will put the fish in a plastic bag with air (or oxygen for long journeys) taking up most of the space in the bag. Keep the bag cool and covered in a brown paper outer or black bin liner, as fish are less stressed in the dark. On long journeys, stand the bag upright inside an insulated polystyrene box, held in place with balls of newspaper. Go straight home; the less time the fish spend in transit, the better they will cope.*

Top right: *Float the bag on the pond with the top tied. After 20 minutes, open the bag and let in some pond water – about half as much as in the bag – and tie the top up again. Leave for another 20 minutes.*

Below right: *Slowly tip the fish and water out into the pond, making sure that all the fish are released. They will hide for a day or two, so there is no need to feed them. After this, feed them once a day at first.*

Checking and maintaining water quality

Once you have set up your pond and introduced any fish, it is important to monitor the water quality. Like all animals, fish need a healthy environment in which to thrive. Because testing sounds complex, it is often overlooked by beginners, but today it is simplicity itself to check the water quality using a range of test kits available from your aquatic dealer.

Whichever test kit you use, keep a record of your results. As you build up the log, it will be easy to spot trends and you will quickly see if a problem is developing. This means that you can take remedial action straight away and be prepared if the same trend develops again. Always buy the same test kit so that you get accustomed to the colours and test procedures. Here we look at the most vital tests. There are others that you can carry out, but they are not essential to start with.

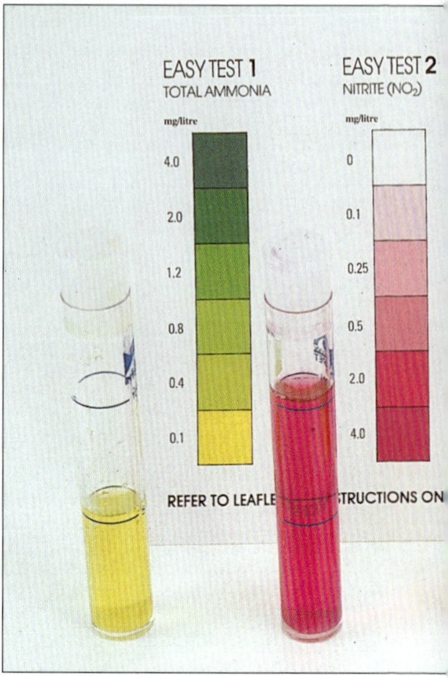

Testing for pH *The pH scale measures the acidity or alkalinity of pond water on a scale from 0 to 14. Extremely acid conditions register as 0, neutral as 7 and a very alkaline reading as 14. Aim for a reading as close as possible to 7. Add one tablet to a water sample, shake the tube, wait and then compare the colour against the chart.*

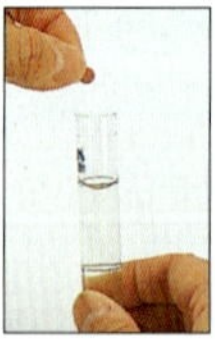

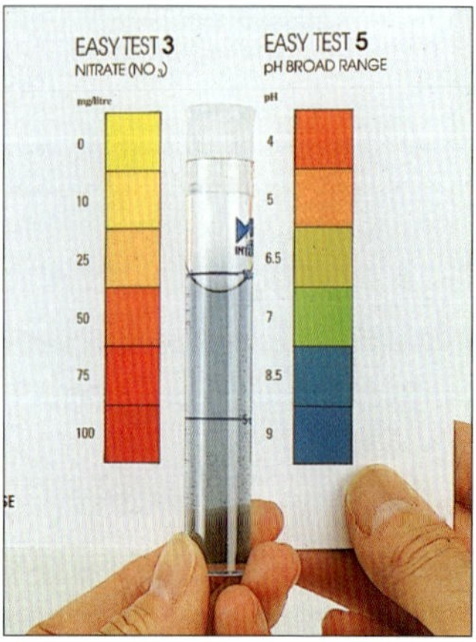

Testing for nitrite *This is the second stage product of the filter system and high levels over a long period can be toxic. To reduce levels quickly, make a water change and stop feeding the fish to give the filter a chance to convert nitrite to nitrate. Test by adding a tablet to a water sample. This test shows a high level of nitrite.*

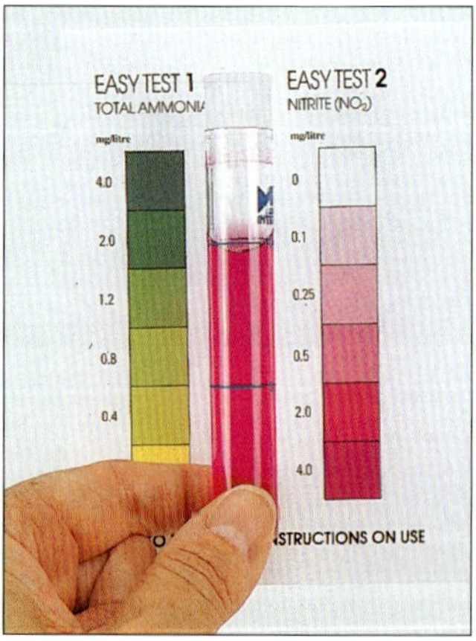

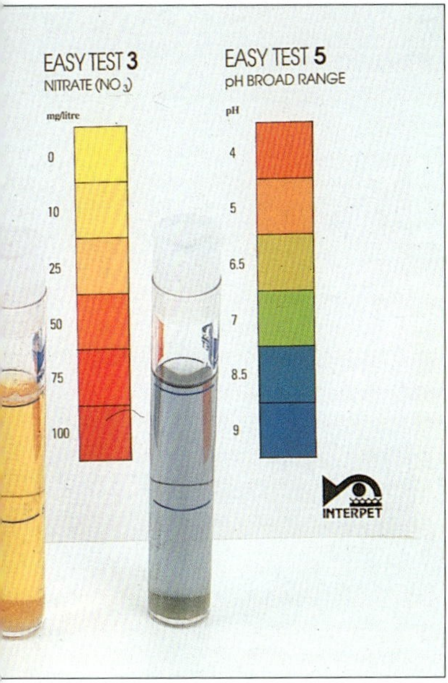

Left: *This range of test kits involves adding tablets to a water sample and comparing the colours to a printed chart. One of the most important tests is for ammonia, especially in a newly set up pond. Ammonia is produced as fish waste decomposes in the water and is also excreted directly by the fish through their gills. Carry out the test once a month and if there is a positive reading, test the water again every day until it is clear.*

Testing for nitrate *The last product in the nitrogen cycle is relatively non-toxic in low levels and is used as plant food. Plants play a vital role, because they use the nitrate to grow. In this two-stage test, the water is already showing a reaction to the first tablet added. The second tablet completes the colour change for the test.*

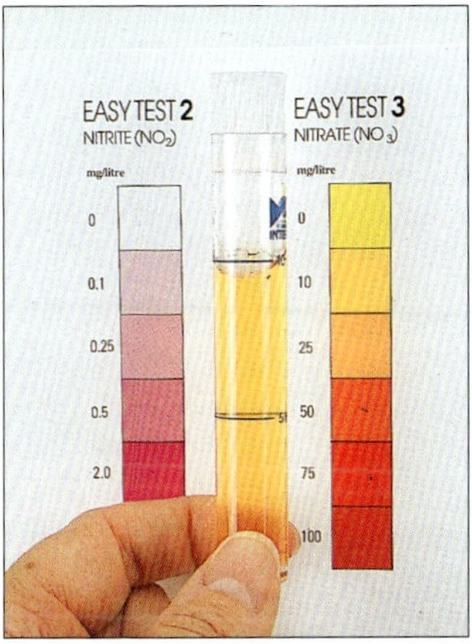

Paper strip test *These test strips enable you to test several water parameters at once. They are supplied in a container with a reference colour chart printed on the label. Take out a strip with dry hands, dip it into the water for one second and remove it. Wait one minute for the colours to develop. Avoid shaking off excess water, which may mix up the results. Do not put used strips with new ones. You can dip the strip directly into the pond or scoop out a cup of water to make the test. Compare the strip colours with the chart. From the top these show nitrate, nitrite, total hardness (three squares), carbonate hardness and pH.*

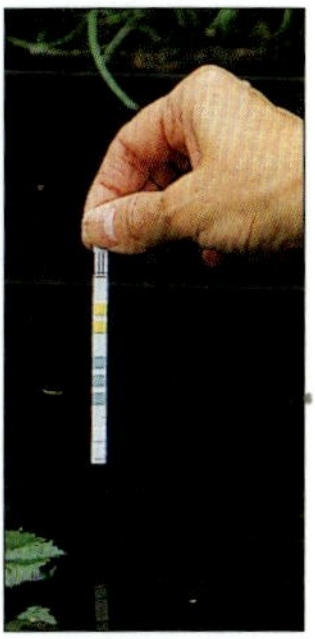

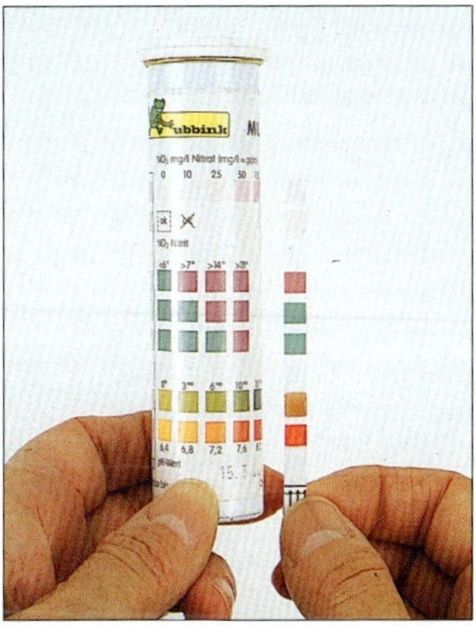

Index to Plants and Fishes

Numbers in *italics* refer to captions. Text entries are shown in normal type.

Picture Credits

Artists

Copyright of the artwork illustrations on the pages following the artists' names is the property of Interpet Publishing.

Clifford and Wendy Meadway: 15, 18(B), 20-1, 25(T), 26, 40, 47, 48, 49, 51, 61
Colin Newman (Linden Artists): 17, 18(T), 19(TL), 30-1, 34-5, 37, 46, 54, 58-9, 64
Tudor Art Studios: 19(TR), 26
Janos Marffy/Eric Tenney: 27

Photographs

The publishers wish to thank the following photographers and agencies who have supplied photographs for this book. The photographs have been credited by page number and position on the page: (B)Bottom, (T)Top, (C)Centre, (BL)Bottom left etc.

MC & C Piednoir/Aqua Press, France: 10-11
Heather Angel/Biofotos: Endpapers, 57(B), 80-81(B), 87(T)
Dave Bevan: 108(B), 109(B)
The British Koi-Keeper's Society: 92(B), 93(T), 95, 96
Bruce Coleman Ltd.: 65(Jane Burton), 68-9(Hans Reinhard), 84-5(Hans Reinhard
Eric Crichton ©Interpet Publishing: 16(B), 23(B), 23(B), 43(B), 51(TL), 93(B)
Bob Essen: 72-3(B), 76-7(T), 77(B), 82(T), 86(B)
Bob Gibbons: 42(C), 43(T)
Jerry Harpur: 37(C)
Neil Holmes: 39
Roger Hyde: 38
Ideas into Print: 72-3(T), 92(T), 94(T), 96-7(B)
Interpet Publishing: 20-21, 22, 23, 25(C), 32-33, 38-39, 44-45, 52-53, 110-111, 112-113
Frank Lane Picture Agency: 100-1(© W Meinderts/Foto Natura)
Jan-Eric Larsson: 74-5(B)
Lotus Water Garden Products Ltd: 45
Dick Mills: 25(B), 41, 45, 55, 56, 57(T), 63, 70-1(B), 71(T), 76(B)
Arend van den Nieuwenhuizen: 62, 78-9, 87(B), 89(B)
Barry Pengilley: Half-title page, title page, copyright page, 16(T), 35, 80(T), 90-1
Laurence Perkins: 28, 66-7, 75(T), 82-3, 88-9(T), 94(B), 96-7(T)
Photomax (Max Gibbs); 78-9, 98-9(B), 102-3, 104-5, 106-7, 108-9(T)
Mike Sandford: 60, 61
Harry Smith Photographic Collection: 42(T)
W A Tomey: 29, 48(BR), 49(B)
P E Whittington: 86(C)

Editorial assistance

Copy-editing by Maureen Cartwright.

Acknowledgements

The publishers would like to thank the following for their assistance in preparing this book: Avi centre, London Ltd.; The British Koi-Keeper's Society; Lotus Water Garden Products Ltd., Burnley; Maclean Marketing Associates; David Quelch, Waterworld.

Common Goldfish